Dr. Birdley Teaches Science!

Elements, Compounds, and Mixtures

Featuring the Comic Strip

Middle and High School

Innovative Resources for the Science Classroom

Written and Illustrated by Nevin Katz

Incentive Publications, Inc.

Nashville, Tennessee

About the Author

Nevin Katz is a teacher and curriculum developer who lives in Amherst, Massachusetts with his wife Melissa and son Jeremy.

Nevin majored in Biology at Swarthmore College and went on to earn his Master's in Education at the Harvard Graduate School of Education. He began developing curriculum as a student teacher in Roxbury, Massachusetts.

"Mr. Katz" has been teaching science over six years, in grades 6 through 11. He currently teaches Biology, Environmental Science, and Physical Science at Ludlow High School in Ludlow, Massachusetts.

Nevin's journey with Dr. Birdley and the cast began in the summer of 2002, when he started authoring the cartoon and using it in his science classes. From there, he developed the cartoon strip, characters, and curriculum materials. After designing and implementing the materials, he decided to develop them further and organize them into a series of books.

Cover by Geoffrey Brittingham

Edited by Jill Norris

Science Editors: K. Noel Freitas and Scott Norris

ISBN 978-0-86530-536-6

1   2   3   4   5   6   7   8   9   10   10   09   08   07

PRINTED IN THE UNITED STATES OF AMERICA

www.incentivepublications.com

TABLE OF CONTENTS

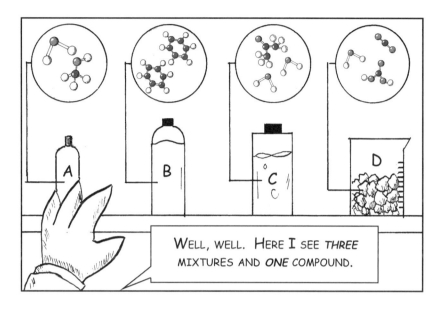

WELL, WELL. HERE I SEE *THREE* MIXTURES AND *ONE* COMPOUND.

Objectives and Frameworks

Central Goal: • To describe the characteristic of elements, compounds, and mixtures
• To relate their properties to the particles they are made up of

Chapter	Primary Objective(s)	Standards
1. The Language of Chemistry	To introduce how symbols and formulas are used to introduce atoms and molecules.	1, 2, 3
2. Elements	To introduce elements as the simplest forms of matter with specific identities, and introduce subatomic particles of atoms.	1, 5
3. Compounds	To introduce and define compounds.	2, 3, 4
4. Compounds & Mixtures	To compare and contrast compounds and mixtures. To compare and contrast homogeneous and heterogeneous mixtures.	2, 3
5. Mendeleev	To describe how Mendeleev developed the periodic table.	1, 7, 8
6. Element Blocks	To understand what the information on the periodic table means about the structure of the atom.	1, 5, 7, 8
7. Subatomic Particles	To describe the mass and charge of an atom's subatomic particles.	1, 5, 6
8. Polar and Nonpolar Molecules	To describe characteristics of polar molecules and nonpolar molecules.	3, 4, 5

National Science Education Standards, Grades 5-8

1. A substance composed of a single kind of atom is called an element.

2. There are more than 100 known elements that combine in a multitude of ways to produce compounds, which account for the living and nonliving substances that we encounter.

3. A compound is formed when two or more kinds of atoms bind together chemically.

4. A substance has characteristic properties, such as density, a boiling point, and solubility, all of which are independent of the amount of the sample.

National Academies Press, 2005
http://www.nap.edu/readingroom/books/nses/

National Science Education Standards, Grades 9-12

5. Matter is made of minute particles called atoms, and atoms are composed of even smaller components. These components have measurable properties, such as mass and electrical charge. Each atom has a positively charged nucleus surrounded by negatively charged electrons.

6. The atom's nucleus is composed of protons and neutrons, which are much more massive than electrons.

7. Substances often are placed in categories or groups if they react in similar ways; metals is an example of such a group.

8. When atoms are listed in order of protons (atomic number) repeating patterns of physical and chemical properties identify families of elements with similar properties.

Overview of Source Cartoons

The difficulty level ranges from easy (L1) to very challenging (L3).

Cartoon	Central Concept	Challenge Level	Related Topics
Symbols & Formulas	Elements are represented by symbols, while compounds are represented by formulas.	L2	Chemical Bonds Molecular Mass
All About Elements	Elements are the smallest units of matter with distinct identities, which are indicated by the atomic number.	L2	Atomic Structure Nuclear Fission
Compound Coolness	Two samples of any compound have the same properties and chemical composition. Compounds can only be broken down through chemical changes.	L2	Chemical Reactions, Hydrolysis of Water
Nano-Goggles	Whereas compounds contain one type of molecule, mixtures contain more than one type of molecule. Elements contain only one type of atom.	L2	Separating of Mixtures
Two Types of Mixtures	Heterogeneous mixtures have unevenly distributed compounds, while homogeneous mixtures contain evenly distributed compounds.	L1	Solutions
Mendeleev (part 1)	Mendeleev, who worked in Russia during the 19th century, was the father of the periodic table.	L1	Aristotle's Elements
Mendeleev (part 2)	By sorting the elements in order of atomic weight, Mendeleev drafted the periodic table.	L2	Purifying Elements
Element Blocks (part 1)	The atomic number and mass number give important information on the atom's structure.	L2	Valence Electrons
Element Blocks (part 2)	Each vertical group of the periodic table has elements with similar properties.	L1	Metals, Non-metals
Subatomic Particles	Atoms are made up of protons, neutrons, and electrons, each with a distinct mass and charge.	L2	Atomic Bonding
A Polar Molecule	Polar molecules have an uneven electron distribution.	L3	Complete vs. Partial Charges
Oil and Water	Oil and Water do not mix because polar and nonpolar molecules avoid each other.	L2	Cell Membranes

Dr. Birdley Teaches Science –
Elements, Compounds, and Mixtures

TEACHER'S GUIDE

Contents

GREETINGS! MY NAME IS DR. BIRDLEY. I AM HERE TO EXPLAIN WHAT THIS BOOK IS ALL ABOUT.

AT FIRST GLANCE, THIS LOOKS LIKE A BOOK OF ENTERTAINING CARTOONS...

WITH HANDSOME CHARACTERS SUCH AS MYSELF.

BUT UPON FURTHER INSPECTION...

EGADS! THESE CARTOONS ARE EDUCATIONAL!

PRECISELY.

THIS BOOK FOCUSES ON THE COMPOSITION OF ELEMENTS, COMPOUNDS, AND MIXTURES.

EACH CARTOON COMES WITH A SET OF RELATED ASSIGNMENTS.

THEY CAN BE USED FOR LESSON TIME,

GROUP ACTIVITIES,

OR DRAMATIC READINGS.

FOLLOW ME, AND I WILL SHOW YOU HOW TO USE THEM!

Dr. Birdley Teaches Science –
Elements, Compounds, and Mixtures

The Source Cartoon

The *Source Cartoon* explains the central concepts of the overall chapter. It is usually one to two pages in length. Expect to find the following in a given source cartoon:

• A central idea with supporting details

• Visual images related to the topic being presented

• Explanations of science concepts

• A range of characters that explain the information to each other or to the reader

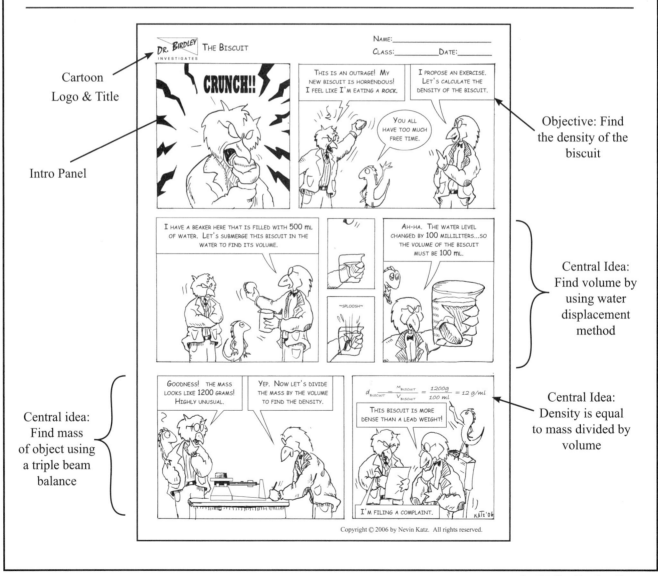

Cartoon Logo & Title

Intro Panel

Objective: Find the density of the biscuit

Central Idea: Find volume by using water displacement method

Central idea: Find mass of object using a triple beam balance

Central Idea: Density is equal to mass divided by volume

The Cartoon Profile

The *Cartoon Profile,* which outlines a source cartoon's science content, is useful for planning or teaching a lesson. Central elements include:

• The objectives in the cartoon, which are listed alongside the related state or national standards.

• The "questions for discussion" below the image, which are useful for getting students engaged and checking for understanding.

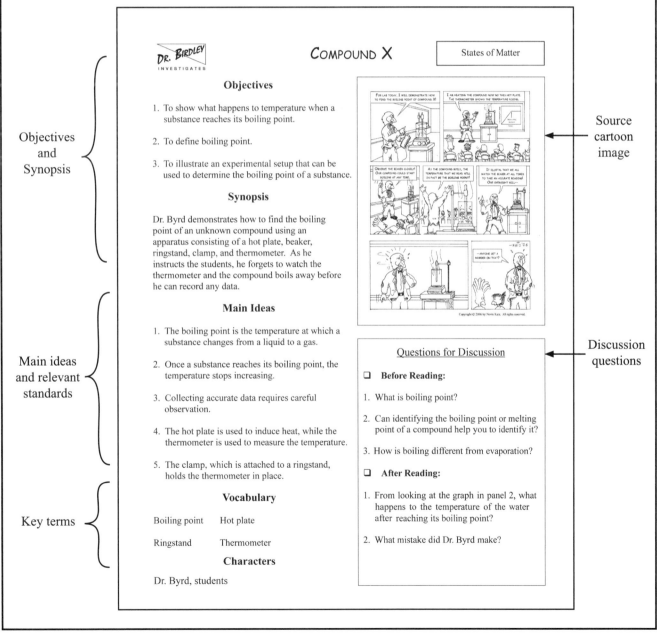

Assignments & Assessments

Supplementary assignments help students build comprehension of the central ideas in the cartoons. While quizzes assess students' knowledge of key points from a given unit. Five of the major assignments in each chapter and one page of a sample section assessment are pictured below:

Study Questions

Visual Exercises

Graphic Organizer

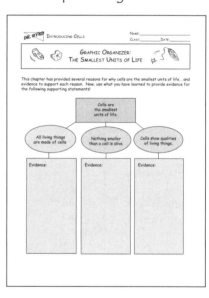

Vocabulary Build-up

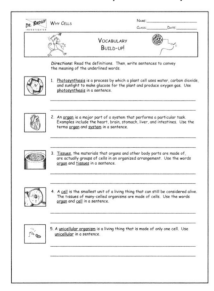

Background Article

Quiz

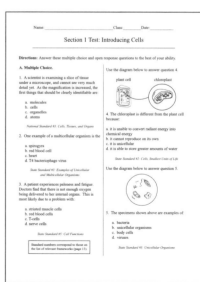

Unit 1: The Language of Chemistry

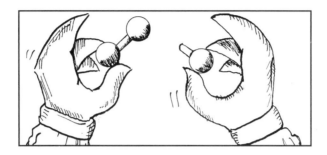

Contents

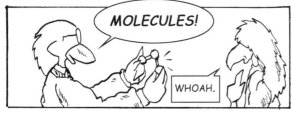

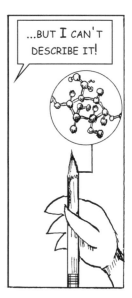

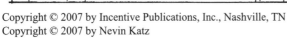

Dr. Birdley Teaches Science –
Elements, Compounds, and Mixtures

SYMBOLS & FORMULAS

Language of Chemistry

Objectives

1. To familiarize students with basic chemistry nomenclature.

2. To illustrate the relevance of chemistry by showing that every-day objects are made of molecules.

3. To illustrate how atoms relate to molecules.

Synopsis

Dr. Birdley finds that Neil, one of his students, is disillusioned with chemistry class and busy doodling. Birdley explains the importance of atomic symbols. He then shows how atoms combine using molecular models and gives Neil special goggles that allow him to see a molecule within his pencil. By the end of the comic, Neil is creating paintings of molecules.

Main Ideas

1. Each atomic symbol stands for a particular type of element, which is composed of a single type of atom.

2. Atoms combine to form molecules.

3. A formula represents a particular type of compound, made of two or more atoms.

4. A formula indicates the number of atoms of each element in the molecule.

Vocabulary

Symbol	atom	element
formula	molecule	compound

Characters

Dr. Birdley and Neil

Questions for Discussion

Before Reading:

1. Why is chemistry important?

2. How do atomic symbols differ from regular letters?

After Reading:

1. What are two teaching strategies Dr. Birdley used?

2. How did Neil's views about chemistry change by the end of the comic?

3. What was the purpose of the goggles? The molecular models?

Dr. Birdley Teaches Science –
Elements, Compounds, and Mixtures

NAME:_____

CLASS:_____DATE:_____

Background: Neil Discusses Symbols & Formulas

Whoa! What a day. There I was, just doodling in chemistry class. Then, Dr. Birdley showed me that chemistry is actually interesting and relevant to real life. Who knew that my pencil was made of molecules?!

Those weird letters are actually symbols for elements...which are specific types of atoms.

Elements, which are all found on the periodic table, are the simplest forms of matter. Atoms are the smallest units of matter.

Atoms combine to form molecules, which can be represented by formulas. Got it? Wait, I should really make some sort of diagram. How about this:

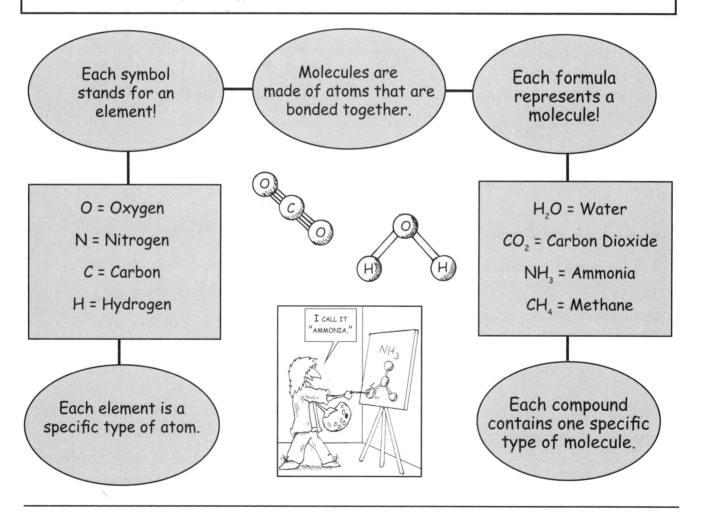

How are atoms and molecules related?

_____

_____

STUDY QUESTIONS

Directions: Answer the following questions to the best of your ability.

 1. What is Neil's opinion about the language of chemistry at the beginning of the comic?

_____

_____

 2. Explain the importance of the symbols that Dr. Birdley points to.

_____

_____

 3. How do atoms relate to molecules? How does Dr. Birdley illustrate this point?

_____

_____

 4. Explain how the goggles help Neil understand the importance of molecules.

_____

_____

 5. What do formulas tell us about molecules?

_____

_____

Dr. Birdley Teaches Science –
Elements, Compounds, and Mixtures

DR. BIRDLEY
INVESTIGATES

MOLECULES & FORMULAS

NAME:_____

CLASS:_____ DATE:_____

WRITE THE FORMULA THAT SHOWS THE **CORRECT NUMBER OF ATOMS** UNDER EACH MOLECULE. USE THE FORMULA BANK!

Water

Acetone

KATZ '04

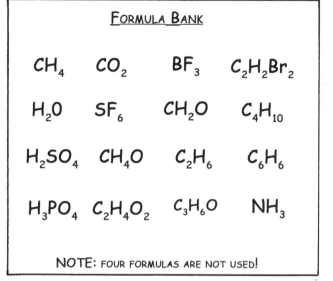

FORMULA BANK

CH_4 CO_2 BF_3 $C_2H_2Br_2$

H_2O SF_6 CH_2O C_4H_{10}

H_2SO_4 CH_4O C_2H_6 C_6H_6

H_3PO_4 $C_2H_4O_2$ C_3H_6O NH_3

NOTE: FOUR FORMULAS ARE NOT USED!

BORON TRIFLOURIDE

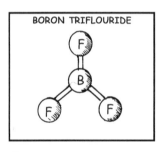

1._____

SULFUR HEXAFLOURIDE

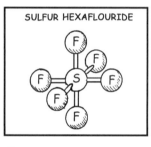

2._____

FORMALDEHYDE

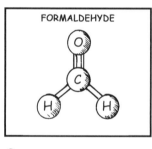

3._____

ACETONE

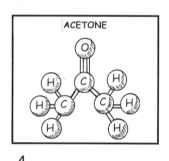

4._____

WATER

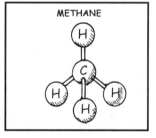

5._____

METHANE

6._____

CARBON DIOXIDE

7._____

DIBROMOETHYLENE

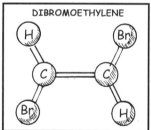

8._____

BENZENE

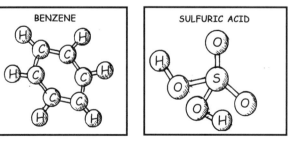

9._____

SULFURIC ACID

10._____

METHANOL

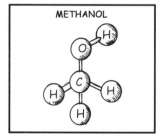

11._____

ETHANE

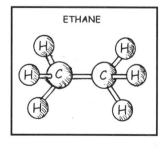

12._____

Dr. Birdley Teaches Science –
Elements, Compounds, and Mixtures

VOCABULARY BUILD-UP!

Directions: Use the following underlined words in meaningful sentences.

1. A <u>molecule</u> is a tiny structure made of atoms bonded together. Atoms are the smallest units of matter. Use <u>molecule</u> and <u>atom</u> in a sentence.

_____

_____

2. A <u>compound</u> is a substance that contains ONE type of molecule. Examples include water and carbon dioxide. Use <u>compound</u> in a sentence.

_____

_____

2 4.0
He
Helium

3. An <u>element</u> is a substance that has ONE specific type of atom. Examples include hydrogen, helium, carbon, and oxygen. Use <u>element</u> in a sentence.

_____

_____

H_2O

4. A <u>formula</u> is a group of symbols that represents a particular element. Examples include H_2O and CO_2. Use <u>formula</u> in a sentence.

_____

_____

K   Rb
Br   I

5. An <u>atomic symbol</u> is one or two letters that represents an element. Examples include H, C, Na. Use <u>atomic symbols</u> in a sentence with two more examples.

_____

_____

Dr. Birdley Teaches Science –
Elements, Compounds, and Mixtures

MINI-COMIC: FINDING MOLECULAR MASS

Directions: Read the panel in the space below and solve the problems that follow.

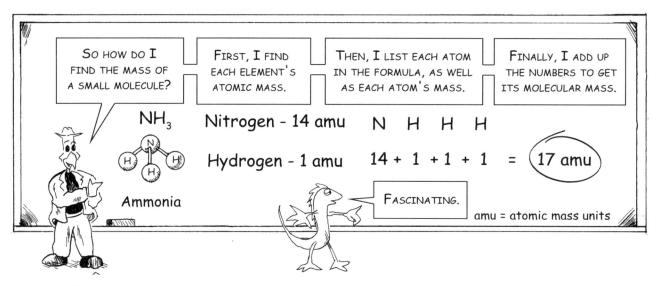

Using the above method, find the molecular mass for each of the following compounds.

1. CH_4

2. CH_2O

3. NaCl

4. NO_2

5. HBr

6. $KMnO_4$

7. H_2SO_4

8. $CaCl_2$

9. $MgCO_3$

10. H_2O_2

Dr. Birdley Teaches Science –
Elements, Compounds, and Mixtures

MINI-COMIC: THE TABLE METHOD

Directions: Read the panel in the space below and solve the problems that follow.

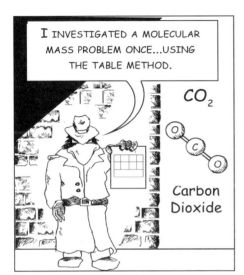
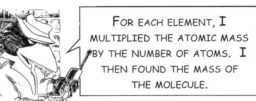

Element Name	Atomic Mass	# atoms	Total mass
Carbon	12	1	12
Oxygen	16	2	32
TOTAL			44

Using the table method, find the molecular masses for the following compounds:

Glucose ($C_6H_{12}O_6$)

Element Name	Atomic Mass	# Atoms	Total Mass
Carbon			
Oxygen			
Hydrogen			
TOTAL			

Acetic Acid ($C_2H_4O_2$)

Element Name	Atomic Mass	# Atoms	Total Mass
Carbon			
Oxygen			
Hydrogen			
TOTAL			

Nitrogen (V) Oxide (N_2O_5)

Element Name	Atomic Mass	# Atoms	Total Mass
Oxygen			
Nitrogen			
TOTAL			

Rust (Fe_2O_3)

Element Name	Atomic Mass	# Atoms	Total Mass
Iron			
Oxygen			
TOTAL			

*Dr. Birdley Teaches Science –
Elements, Compounds, and Mixtures*

Name:_____ Class:_____ Date:_____

Unit 1 Quiz

Directions: This quiz tests your knowledge of the chapter's cartoon, background article, and visual exercises. Answer the following questions to the best of your ability.

1. Which of the following models correctly represents the compound acetic acid ($C_2H_4O_2$)?

   a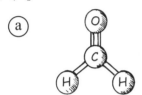

   b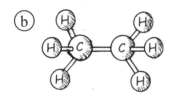

   c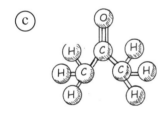

   d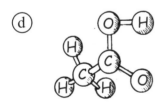

2. All elements are commonly represented by:
   - (a) molecular masses
   - (b) symbols
   - (c) formulas
   - (d) single letters

3. A scientist reacts hydrogen gas with nitrogen gas to form ammonia (NH_3). This combination illustrates that ammonia is:
   - (a) an atom
   - (b) an element
   - (c) a mixture
   - (d) a compound

4. The molecular mass for methane (CH_4) is:
   - (a) 12 amu
   - (b) 4 amu
   - (c) 16 amu
   - (d) 8 amu

5. Use the table method below to find the mass of acetone (C_3H_6O):

Element Name	Atomic Mass	# Atoms	Total Mass
Carbon			
Oxygen			
Hydrogen			
TOTAL			

6. Molecules are made up of _____ bonded together.
   - (a) protons
   - (b) atoms
   - (c) neutrons
   - (d) electrons

Dr. Birdley Teaches Science –
Elements, Compounds, and Mixtures

Unit 2: All About Elements

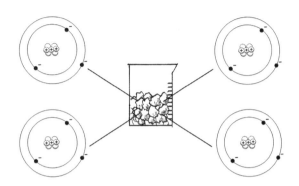

Contents

Dr. Birdley Teaches Science –
Elements, Compounds, and Mixtures

NAME:_____

CLASS:_____DATE:_____

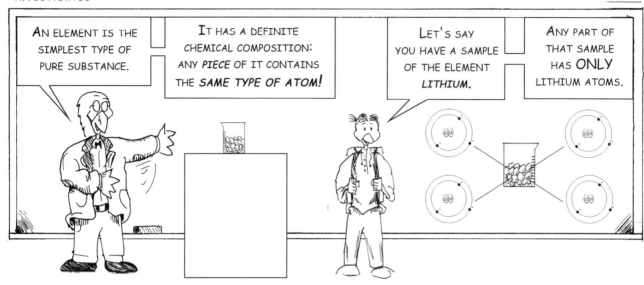

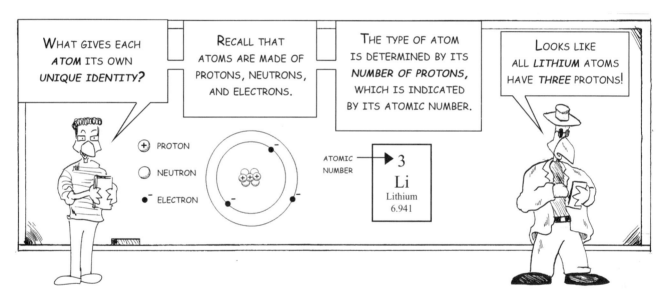

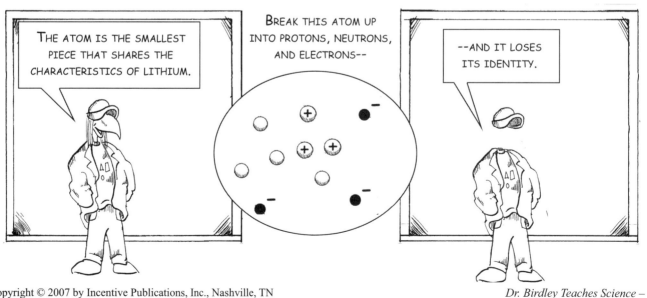

Dr. Birdley Teaches Science –
Elements, Compounds, and Mixtures

Objectives

1. To explain the significance of protons and the atomic number.

2 To explain how elements are related to atoms.

3. To show that the atom is as the smallest unit of matter with a unique identity.

Synopsis

A group of students explain what makes an element and its atoms unique.

Main Ideas

1. A pure sample of any element consists of only one type of atom.

2. An atom is made up of protons, neutrons, and electrons.

3. The type of element is determined by the number of protons, which is indicated by the atomic number.

4 If an atom is broken into protons, neutrons, and electrons, it loses its identity.

Vocabulary

Element	protons	electrons
atom	neutrons	atomic number

Characters

Dr. Birdley and Neil

Questions for Discussion

Before Reading:

1. What are examples of elements you can think of?

2. How do you think elements are different from other types of substances?

After Reading:

1. Why did Greg disappear?

2. Are atoms the smallest units of matter?

3. How do we know the sample of lithium at the top of the cartoon is an element?

Dr. Birdley Teaches Science –
Elements, Compounds, and Mixtures

Background: All About Elements

7 Main Ideas

1. Elements are substances that are composed of only one type of atom!

2. Elements can be considered the simplest, purest forms of matter.

3. Atoms can be thought of as the smallest units of matter with specific identities.

4. An atom is made up of smaller particles called subatomic particles.

5. There are three types of subatomic particles: protons, neutrons, and electrons.

6. An atom's identity is determined by its number of protons

7. If an atom is broken up into subatomic particles, it loses its identity. That means that an atom will not have the same chemical properties if it is broken into subatomic particles.

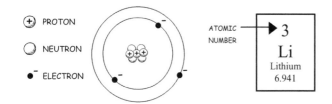

⊕ PROTON
◯ NEUTRON
• ELECTRON

ATOMIC NUMBER → 3
Li
Lithium
6.941

Helpful Formulas

Atomic # = Number of Protons

(In neutral atoms, the atomic number is also equal to the number of electrons.)

Mass # = # Protons + # Neutrons

So,

neutrons = Mass # - Atomic

Using a periodic table, fill out the chart below with the correct information. Assume that all the elements are neutral.

Element	Atomic Number	Mass Number	Number of Protons	Number of Neutrons	Number of Electrons
Hydrogen					
Carbon					
Nitrogen					
Lithium					
Helium					
Fluorine					

Dr. Birdley Teaches Science –
Elements, Compounds, and Mixtures

ALL ABOUT ELEMENTS

Name:_____
Class:_____Date:_____

STUDY
QUESTIONS

Directions: After reading the cartoon, answer the questions that follow.

1. How is an element different from a compound or mixture?

_____

_____

2. What three particles are atoms composed of?
   How are atoms different?

_____

_____

3. Why is the number of protons important? What information in the
   box tells you the number of protons in an atom?

_____

_____

6
C
CARBON
12.0

4. Use your periodic table. If Lithium has only three protons, how many
   protons does carbon have?   How do you know this?

_____

_____

5. What happens to the atom if it is broken apart?

_____

_____

Dr. Birdley Teaches Science –
Elements, Compounds, and Mixtures

Name:_____
Class:_____Date:_____

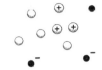

VOCABULARY
BUILD-UP!

Directions: Use the following underlined words in meaningful sentences.

1. An <u>element</u> is the simplest type of pure substance. It is made up of only one type of atom. Use <u>element</u> in sentence.

_____

_____

2. An <u>atom</u> is the smallest unit of an element that retains all its properties. Use <u>atom</u> in a sentence.

_____

_____

3. The <u>proton</u> is the positively charged particle of the atom. The number of protons in an atom is shown by its atomic number. Use the word <u>proton</u> in a sentence.

_____

_____

4. The <u>neutrons</u> are the neutral particles in the atom – particles with no electric charge. Use <u>neutron</u> in a sentence.

_____

_____

5. The <u>electrons</u> are the negatively charged parts of the atom that fly around the nucleus. Use <u>electron</u> in a sentence.

_____

_____

Dr. Birdley Teaches Science –
Elements, Compounds, and Mixtures

Unit 3: Compounds

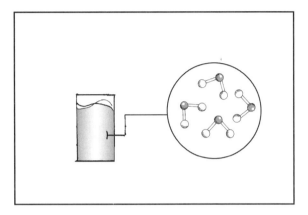

Contents

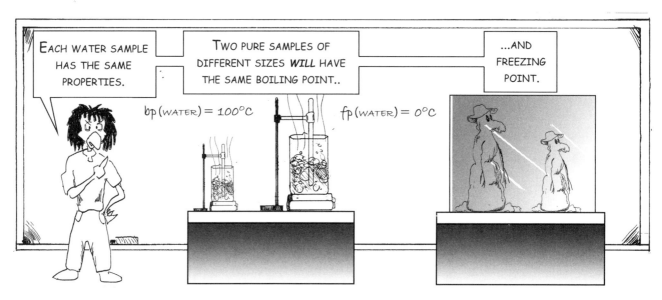

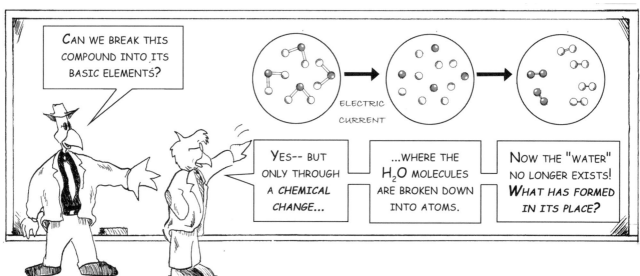

Dr. Birdley Teaches Science –
Elements, Compounds, and Mixtures

Compound Coolness

Objectives

1. To point out what defines a pure substance.

2. To illustrate what a pure substance looks like at the molecular level.

3. To provide an illustration of what happens to molecules during a chemical reaction.

Synopsis

Dr. Birdley begins to explain concepts behind pure substances, but his students and colleagues take over!

Main Ideas

1. Compounds have a definite chemical composition.

2. Any two samples of a pure substance will have the same physical properties, regardless of size.

3. Compounds can only be broken down into elements by chemical changes.

4. At the end of the comic, water is broken down chemically to form oxygen and hydrogen gas.

Vocabulary

Compound   melting point   molecules

chemical change   freezing point

Characters

Dr. Birdley, Norman, Neil, Anita, Jaykes, and Dean Owelle.

Copyright © 2005 by Nevin Katz. All rights reserved.

Questions for Discussion

Before Reading:

1. What does the term "pure" mean?

2. What would you need to know to tell if a substance is pure?

After Reading:

1. What is required to break a compound into elements?

2. Two snowmen have the same melting point, but the smaller one melts faster. Does this mean the melting point is still the same or not?

3. What's an example of a pure substance you might run into in everyday life?

Dr. Birdley Teaches Science –
Elements, Compounds, and Mixtures

NAME:_____

CLASS:_____DATE:_____

Background: Compound Coolness

The following is an excerpt from the journal of Norman the lizard:

Boy. That Birdley really struggles to explain something without big words. The bottom line is this: compounds contain ONE type of molecule only.

The second point is that they have the same basic properties, regardless of size or shape: the same boiling point, melting point, density, or shape.

Finally, compounds can't be broken down by ordinary means. Boiling, spinning, and filtering just doesn't work with these things. It will only make their molecules jump around a bit more.

To break down compounds you must use chemical reactions...the bonds that hold the molecules together are broken up and then reform.

Birdley showed an example of the electrolysis of water, where water molecules (H_2O) are broken down and form the atoms for oxygen gas (O_2) and hydrogen gas (H_2).

What did I learn? Pure substances consist of one type of molecule, their properties stay the same regardless of size or shape, and they can only be broken down by chemical reactions. Now if only Birdley could explain things as clearly as that.

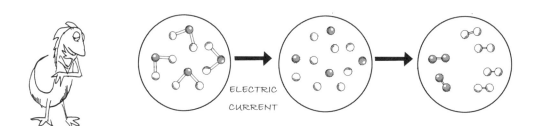

Directions: Explain the major points about compounds that are mentioned in the comic.

_____

_____

_____

_____

Dr. Birdley Teaches Science –
Elements, Compounds, and Mixtures

 STUDY QUESTIONS

Directions: Read the related cartoon and answer the following questions.

1. Explain the meaning of the statement, "Every compound has a definite chemical composition."

_____

_____

2. What are two physical properties that do not depend on size? What do they depend on?

_____

_____

3. How can a compound such as water be broken down into its basic elements?

_____

_____

4. What happens to the bonds between atoms during a chemical reaction? What is the result of this process?

_____

_____

5. How are compounds different from elements?

_____

_____

Dr. Birdley Teaches Science –
Elements, Compounds, and Mixtures

COMPOUNDS: LINKING IMAGES

IN THE SPACE BETWEEN EACH SET OF IMAGES, WRITE A LINKING PHRASE TO CREATE A FACTUAL SENTENCE. USE THE PHRASE BANK!

PHRASE BANK

CANNOT BE BROKEN DOWN THROUGH

IS MADE OF ONLY ONE TYPE OF

CAN ONLY BE BROKEN DOWN USING

OF THE SAME COMPOUND HAVE THE SAME

CAN COMBINE TO FORM A

A COMPOUND _____ MOLECULE

TWO SAMPLES _____ FREEZING POINT

WATER _____ CHEMICAL CHANGES

CITRIC ACID _____ PHYSICAL CHANGES

ELEMENTS _____ COMPOUND

Dr. Birdley Teaches Science –
Elements, Compounds, and Mixtures

DR. BIRDLEY
INVESTIGATES

COMPOUND COOLNESS

Name:_____
Class:_____Date:_____

 VOCABULARY
BUILD-UP!

Directions: Use each underlined word in an original sentence that conveys its meaning.

1. A <u>sample</u> is a small portion of a substance that a scientist examines to learn more about the whole substance. You might take a sample of river water to learn about the amount of river pollution. Use <u>sample</u> in a sentence.

_____

_____

2. <u>Composition</u> describes what a substance is made of. For example, water is made of oxygen and hydrogen. Use <u>composition</u> in a meaningful sentence.

_____

_____

3. A <u>chemical change</u> is a chemical reaction that is needed to break a compound down into its basic elements. When water is broken down, hydrogen and oxygen gas are formed. Use <u>chemical change</u> in a sentence.

_____

_____

4. A <u>physical change</u> could be melting, freezing, boiling, breaking, or filtering... any change that does not change one substance into another substance. Use <u>physical change</u> in a sentence.

_____

_____

5. The <u>boiling point</u> is the temperature at which a pure substance boils. If the substance is pure, the boiling point stays the SAME, regardless of size. The boiling point of water is always 100°C. Use <u>boiling point</u> in a sentence.

_____

_____

Dr. Birdley Teaches Science –
Elements, Compounds, and Mixtures

Unit 4: The Composition of Matter

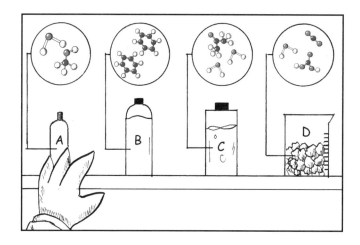

Contents

NAME:_____

CLASS:_____DATE:_____

MINI-COMIC: COMPOSITION OF MATTER

Directions: Review the panel in the space below and answer the questions that follow.

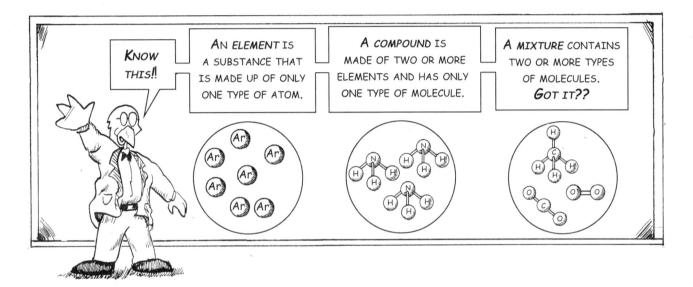

1. What is the difference between a compound and an element?

2. What is the difference between a compound and a mixture?

3. Can mixtures be represented by formulas?   Why or why not?

4. Is the mixture shown a solid, liquid, or gas?   How do you know?

5. List all the elements shown in the mini-comic above.

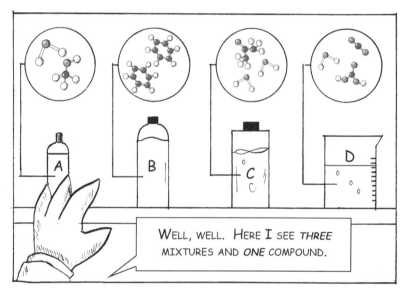

Dr. Birdley Teaches Science –
Elements, Compounds, and Mixtures

NANO-GOGGLES

Compounds and Mixtures

Objectives

1. To show how compounds and mixtures differ at the molecular level.

2. To provide an exercise where students must identify the pure substance based on its constituent molecules.

Synopsis

Dr. Birdley demonstrates the nano-goggles, which allow one to see the molecules that an object or substance is made up of. He uses the goggles to identify the composition of Owelle's drink and four laboratory reagents. Baby Birdley is using the goggles to identify the composition of water in a cup.

Main Ideas

1. Mixtures are made up of more than one type of molecule.

2. Compounds, which are pure substances, contain only contain one type of molecule but two or more types of elements.

3. Mixtures are not pure substances.

4. The molecules visible in Owelle's soda are water and carbon dioxide.

Vocabulary

Compound   pure substance

mixture   molecules

Characters

Dr. Birdley, Dean Owelle, Baby Birdley

Questions for Discussion

Before Reading:

1. What is the difference between a compound and a mixture?

2. Is soda a compound or a mixture?

After Reading:

1. Which of the four laboratory reagents was the compound? How could you tell?

2. What is the difference between a pure substance and a mixture?

3. What was Owelle's soda made of?

4. What was Baby Birdley looking at through the goggles?

Dr. Birdley Teaches Science –
Elements, Compounds, and Mixtures

TWO TYPES OF MIXTURES | Compounds and Mixtures

Objectives

1 To visually distinguish between homogenous and heterogeneous mixtures.

2. To provide an exercise where students must identify the pure substance based on its constituent molecules.

Synopsis

Dr. Birdley, Owelle, Jaykes, and some students are admiring Neil's painting, which illustrates two jars, each with a different type of mixture.

Main Ideas

1. Mixtures are made up of more than one type of molecule.

2. In the jar on the left, the molecules are unevenly distributed (heterogeneous).

3. In the jar on the right, the molecules are evenly distributed (homogenous.)

Vocabulary

Solution   heterogeneous

mixture   homogenous

Characters

Dr. Birdley, Dean Owelle, Jaykes, Neil, Students, Dept. of Education Representative

Questions for Discussion

Before Reading:

1. What are three examples of everyday mixtures?

2. Why do you need to shake and stir mixtures?

After Reading:

1. If this painting was drawn to scale, how big do you think the jars would have to be?

2. Which mixture is heterogeneous? Homogenous?

3. What do you think the molecules are?

Dr. Birdley Teaches Science –
Elements, Compounds, and Mixtures

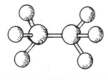 STUDY QUESTIONS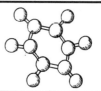

Directions: Answer the following questions to the best of your ability.

 1. Describe the powers that Dr. Birdley's goggles have.

_____

_____

 2. How does Dr. Birdley demonstrate these powers to Dean Owelle?

_____

_____

 3. In the lab cabinet, which substance (A, B, C, or D) is a compound? How is it different from the other three mixtures?

_____

_____

 4. What do you think makes compounds "pure" and mixtures "impure"?

_____

_____

 5. How could Birdley's goggles be used in a science-related job? (Building houses, designing cars, creating medications...pick your favorite.)

_____

_____

Dr. Birdley Teaches Science – Elements, Compounds, and Mixtures

TWO TYPES OF MIXTURES

Name:_____
Class:_____Date:_____

 Study Questions

Directions: Answer the following questions to the best of your ability.

1. In science, <u>heterogeneous</u> refers to unevenly distributed particles. In Neil's painting, which jar was heterogeneous? How can you tell?

_____

_____

_____

2. In science, <u>homogeneous</u> refers to evenly distributed particles. In Neil's painting, which jar was homogenous? How can you tell?

_____

_____

_____

3. Which jar reveals the relative densities of the compounds? How can you tell?

_____

_____

_____

4. How could you make the mixture on the left become more like the mixture on the right? Explain.

_____

_____

_____

Dr. Birdley Teaches Science –
Elements, Compounds, and Mixtures

NAME:_____

CLASS:_____ DATE:_____

Background: Nano-Goggles, Two Types of Mixtures, Solutions

The goal of "The Nano-Goggles" is to illustrate how compounds and mixtures differ at the molecular level.

Dr. Birdley's goggles allow him to zoom in on a substance and see its composition. In the lab cabinet, bottle a, c, and d contain mixtures; and bottle b contains a compound because it has the same type of molecule (see below.)

Water (H_2O)
Ethanol (CH_4O)

Benzene (C_6H_6)

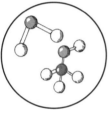 

Water (H_2O)
Acetone(C_3H_6O)

Water (H_2O)
Carbon Dioxide (CO_2)

In "Two Types of Mixtures," Neil's painting depicts a heterogeneous mixture on the left and a homogenous mixture on the right.

Heterogeneous   Homogenous

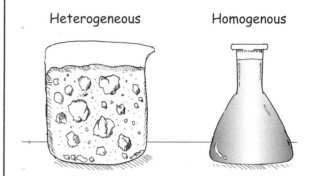

The heterogeneous mixture could be made up of a variety of substances, such as soil and different types of rocks. It is heterogeneous because the various substances are not evenly distributed throughout the mixture. A homogeneous mixture would have a smoother appearance, suggesting that the materials are distributed evenly.

Another type of homogeneous mixture is a solution, where one substance is dissolved in another substance. One example is a salt water solution. If too much salt is added, then some salt remains undissolved and settles at the bottom. In this case, the solution is supersaturated.

What is the difference between a compound and a mixture?

_____

_____

_____

_____

Dr. Birdley Teaches Science –
Elements, Compounds, and Mixtures

 VOCABULARY BUILD-UP!

Directions: Use the following underlined words in meaningful sentences.

 1. Carbon dioxide is a compound that has the formula CO_2. It makes the bubbles in soda water. Use carbon dioxide in a sentence.

_____

_____

 2. A compound is a type of pure substance that contains only one type of molecule. Use compound in a sentence!

_____

_____

 3. An element is a substance that has ONE specific type of atom. Examples include hydrogen, helium, carbon, and oxygen. Use element in a sentence.

_____

_____

 4. A pure substance is either an element or compound. It must contain only ONE type of molecule, or ONE type of atom. Use pure substance in a sentence.

_____

_____

 5. A mixture is NOT a pure substance. It contains more than one type of molecule. Soda, juice, salt water, and other everyday substances are mixtures. Use the term mixture in a sentence.

_____

_____

Dr. Birdley Teaches Science –
Elements, Compounds, and Mixtures

DR. BIRDLEY INVESTIGATES

ELEMENT, COMPOUND, OR MIXTURE?

NAME:_____

CLASS:_____ DATE:_____

CLASSIFY EACH SET OF PARTICLES AS AN ELEMENT, COMPOUND, OR MIXTURE. USE THE CLUES TO THE RIGHT!

CLUES

AN ELEMENT CONTAINS ONLY ONE TYPE OF ATOM.

A COMPOUND CONTAINS ONE TYPE OF MOLECULE. THIS MOLECULE HAS TWO OR MORE TYPES OF ATOMS.

A MIXTURE CONTAINS:

- TWO OR MORE TYPES OF MOLECULES, OR

- ONE TYPE OF MOLECULE AND ANOTHER SEPARATE TYPE OF ATOM.

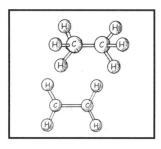

1._____

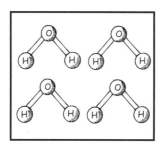

2._____

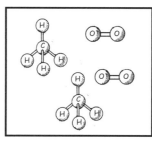

3._____

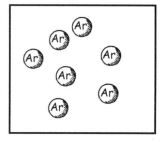

4._____

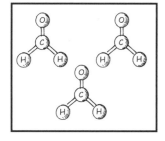

5._____

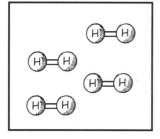

6._____

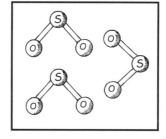

7._____

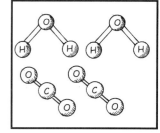

8._____

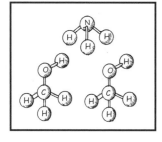

9._____

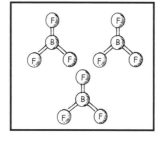

10._____

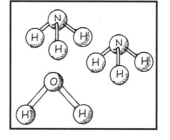

11._____

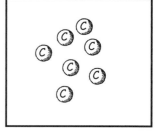

12._____

Dr. Birdley Teaches Science –
Elements, Compounds, and Mixtures

DR. BIRDLEY
INVESTIGATES

NAME:_____

CLASS:_____ DATE:_____

MINI-COMIC: SOLUTIONS

Directions: Read the panel in the space below and answer the questions that follow.

A solution is a mixture in which one substance (a solute) is dissolved in another substance (a solvent.) A solute dissolves when its particles become completely mixed with the particles of the solvent. In this case, Gina is looking for solution of salt (NaCl) dissolved in water (H_2O).

Salt dissolves well in water, but solvents have their limits! You can only dissolve so much of a solute in the solvent. When the maximum amount of dissolved solute is reached, the solution becomes saturated. If more solute is added, it remains undissolved. In this case, the solution is supersaturated.

1. In salt water, what is the solute?_____ What is the solvent?_____

2. What does it mean when a solution becomes saturated?

3. Which solution is supersaturated: A or B? How can you tell?

4. What would you do to this solution to make sure that all of the solute dissolves?

Dr. Birdley Teaches Science –
Elements, Compounds, and Mixtures

Graphic Organizer: Elements, Compounds, and Mixtures

Directions: Sort the substances into the table below. Then, list ten of your own substances in the correct columns.

Elements	Compounds	Mixtures

SUBSTANCE BANK

Helium
Calcium Carbonate
Acetone
Formaldehyde
Nickel
Salt Water
Boron
Vinegar

Chalk
Mud
Clay
Hydrogen Gas
Pond water
Sodium Acetate
Glucose Solution
Cookie Dough

Lithium Chloride
Baking Soda
Nitrogen
Mercury
Acid Rain
Iodine
Taco Sauce
Acetic Acid

NAME:_____

CLASS:_____DATE:_____

 Concept Map: Matter

Fill in the bubbles with the words from the word bank.   Use the Mini-Comic, Source Cartoons, and related background section from this chapter as source material.

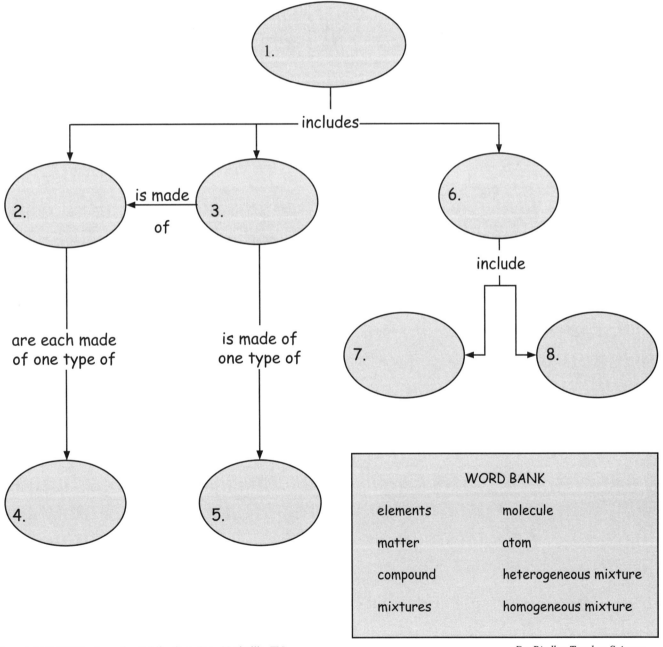

*Dr. Birdley Teaches Science –
Elements, Compounds, and Mixtures*

Unit 4 Quiz

Directions: This quiz tests your knowledge of the chapter's cartoon, background article, and visual exercises. Answer the following questions to the best of your ability.

1. Identify each as an element, compound, or mixture.

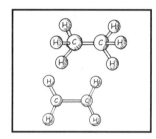 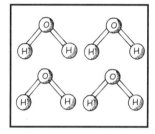 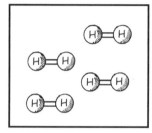 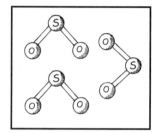

   a. _____   b. _____   c. _____   d. _____

2. Identify each as a mixture (M), element (E), or compound (C).

a. carbon dioxide ____	d. sodium carbonate ____	g. hydrogen ____
b. soda ____	e. carbon ____	h. acetic acid ____
c. neon ____	f. orange juice ____	i. vinegar ____

3. Salt has settled at the bottom of a glass of water. Will stirring the mixture make it become more heterogeneous or homogenous? Why?

4.   Label each mixture as heterogeneous or homogeneous.

   a._____   b._____

Unit 5: Mendeleev & The Periodic Table

Contents

MENDELEEV, PART 1

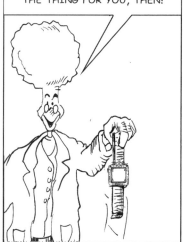

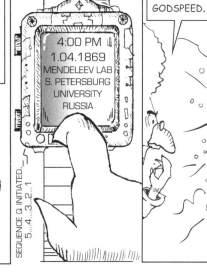

Dr. Birdley Teaches Science –
Elements, Compounds, and Mixtures

Dr. Birdley Teaches Science –
Elements, Compounds, and Mixtures

MENDELEEV, PART 1

Objectives

1. To establish Mendeleev's importance in history.

2. To establish the time and place of Mendeleev.

3. To provoke further thought as to what Mendeleev did and did not know in 1869.

Synopsis

Using a time machine, Birdley travels back in time to visit Mendeleev, the father of the periodic table.

Main Ideas

1. Dimitri Mendeleev came up with the periodic table.

2. Mendeleev lived mainly during the 19th century and worked at the University of St. Petersburg in Russia.

3. By 1869, Mendeleev had analyzed over 44 elements.

Vocabulary

elements   periodic table

Characters

Dr. Birdley, Professor Lark, Dimitri Mendeleev

Teacher's Note: This is primarily a "set-up" cartoon for Mendeleev, Part 2. The included study questions are designed to get students thinking about Mendeleev and his importance in history.

Questions for Discussion

Before Reading:

1. What do you think people knew about the elements in 1869?

2. Who is Mendeleev? Why is he important?

3. What is the periodic table? Why is it important?

After Reading:

1. Do you think Birdley will get the job? Why or why not?

2. Why do you think Dr. Birdley wants to visit Mendeleev?

Dr. Birdley Teaches Science –
Elements, Compounds, and Mixtures

MENDELEEV, PART 2

Objectives

1. To illustrate how Mendeleev collected and organized information on the elements.

2. To introduce the concept of periodicity by discussing the repetitious pattern in the properties across each row in the periodic table.

3. To illustrate how Mendeleev's periodic table in 1869 was different than the modern periodic table.

Synopsis

Dr. Birdley impresses Mendeleev with his knowledge of how he designed the periodic table.

Main Ideas

1. Mendeleev purified and isolated over 44 elements by 1869. (He would ultimately collect data on 63 elements.)

2. Mendeleev recorded the data of each element on a note card.

3. Mendeleev arranged the note cards in order of atomic mass and discovered a pattern.

4. Mendeleev found that if he formed separate rows, each row of elements showed a similar trend in the variation of properties.

5. The periodic table is "periodic" because the variation in elements' properties within a given property shows up again in subsequent periods.

Vocabulary

periodic   atomic weight   properties

Characters

Dr. Birdley, Mendeleev

Questions for Discussion

Before Reading:

1. What is a physical property? Give three examples.

2. What are some ways of purifying a substance?

3. What does the term "periodic" mean? (What does it mean if it is raining periodically during the day?)

After Reading:

1. Why did Mendeleev hire Dr. Birdley?

2. Is it possible to simulate Mendeleev's research process in the classroom? How?

Dr. Birdley Teaches Science – Elements, Compounds, and Mixtures

MENDELEEV, PART 1

Name:_____
Class:_____Date:_____

Study Questions

Directions: Read the related source cartoon and then answer
the questions that follow.

 1. Who is Dimitri Mendeleev? Where did he conduct his work?

_____

_____

 2. What had Mendeleev accomplished by 1869? Why do you think Birdley
considered this a significant time?

_____

_____

 3. Why would Mendeleev's periodic table be smaller than the one we
know today?

_____

_____

 4. Given the time period he lived in, what is on thing about chemistry
that Mendeleev did NOT know while conducting his research?

_____

_____

 5. If you could visit him, what are two chemistry-related questions you
would ask Mendeleev?

_____

_____

Dr. Birdley Teaches Science –
Elements, Compounds, and Mixtures

Name:_____
Class:_____Date:_____

Study Questions

Directions: Read the related source cartoon and then answer
the questions that follow.

1. What did Mendeleev need to do in the lab in order to collect data on an element?

_____

_____

2. Describe how Mendeleev organized the elements.

_____

_____

3. What pattern did Mendeleev find while organizing information on the elements?

_____

_____

	I	II	III
1	H		
2	Li	Be	B
3	Na	Mg	Al

4. What makes the periodic table periodic?

_____

_____

6
C
12.001

5. How is the organization of Mendeleev's periodic table different from that of the modern periodic table?

_____

_____

Dr. Birdley Teaches Science –
Elements, Compounds, and Mixtures

Background: Mendeleev's Table

Dmitri Mendeleev (1834-1907) is known today as the father of the periodic table. Although he did not design the one we know today, he came up with the principle of a table that puts the elements in a deliberate order and groups them according to their properties.

By 1868, Mendeleev had purified and isolated many elements over time. For each element, he had recorded its properties, such as density, reactivity, and melting point, on a single note card. Although he did not know about the atomic number, he arranged the element cards in order of atomic mass.

Mendeleev had found that if he arranged the elements in rows, each row had a similar sequence of element types and variation in properties that showed up. Because there was periodic repetition of element properties in each row, Mendeleev called this the periodic table. Mendeleev also found that the pattern of properties was similar for each vertical group. He presented these findings in 1869.

Because not all the elements had been discovered in his time, Mendeleev's periodic table had some

	I	II	III	IV	V	VI	VII	VIII
1	H							
2	Li	Be	B	C	N	O	F	
3	Na	Mg	Al	Si	P	S	Cl	
4	K Cu	Ca Zn		Ti	V As	Cr Se	Mn Br	Fe Co Ni
5	Rb Ag	Sr Cd	Y In	Zr Sn	Nb Sb	Mo Te	I	Ru Rh Pd

Mendeleev's Periodic Table in 1869.

gaps. The invisible inert gases had not been discovered yet. However, Mendeleev was able to predict the properties of elements he had not yet discovered based on the properties of the other known elements in that group. One of these elements was gallium, which Mendeleev had tentatively named eka-aluminum.

Mendeleev revised his periodic table as more elements were discovered. His most developed periodic table had 63 elements. Today's periodic table has 110 elements, and instead being arranged by atomic mass, our elements are arranged by atomic number.

1. Describe the steps Mendeleev went through in designing the periodic table?_____

_____

_____

2. How is the modern periodic table different from Mendeleev's periodic table?_____

_____

_____

Dr. Birdley Teaches Science –
Elements, Compounds, and Mixtures

MENDELEEV'S TABLE IN 1869

FILL IN MY PERIODIC TABLE AND THEN
ANSWER THE QUESTIONS THAT FOLLOW!
USE THE ELEMENT BANK!

ELEMENT BANK

USING THE ATOMIC MASSES OF THE SAMPLES, FIND
THE AVERAGE MASS OF EACH ELEMENT TO DETERMINE
WHERE IT BELONGS.

BERYLLIUM (Be) MASSES: 5.94, 7.94_____

OXYGEN (O) MASSES: 15.8, 16.1, 16.1_____

NITROGEN (N) MASSES: 13.5, 14.2, 14.3_____

CHLORINE (Cl) MASSES: 34.5, 36.5_____

SILVER (Ag) MASSES: 108, 109, 107_____

	I	II	III	IV	V	VI	VII	VIII
1	H 1.01							
2	Li 4.00	____ ____	B 9.01	C 12.0	____	____	F 19.0	
3	Na 23.0	Mg 24.3	Al 27.0	Si 26.1	P 31.0	S 32.1	____ ____	
4	K 39.1	Ca 40.1	'	Ti 47.9	V 50.9	Cr 52.0	Mn 54.9	Fe Co Ni
	Cu 63.5	Zn 65.4	'	'	As 74.9	Se 79.0	Br 79.9	
5	Rb 85.5	Sr 87.5	Y 88.9	Zr 91.2	Nb 92.9	Mo 95.9	Tc 99	Rn Rh Pd
	____ ____	Cd 112	In 115	Sn 119	Sb 122	Te 126	I 127	

List two metals that you found: _____

List three non-metals you found: _____

Dr. Birdley Teaches Science –
Elements, Compounds, and Mixtures

Vocabulary Build-up!

Directions: Read the related source cartoon and then answer the questions that follow.

1. To <u>isolate</u> a substance is to separate out all the impurities so only the pure substance remains. Use the term <u>isolate</u> in a sentence.

_____

_____

2. The term <u>periodic</u> means regularly repetitious. Use the term <u>periodic</u> in a sentence.

_____

_____

3. <u>Atomic weight</u>, today referred to as atomic mass, is the weight of a single element. Use <u>atomic weight</u> in a sentence.

_____

_____

i	Be	B	C	N
a	Mg	Al	Si	
	Ca	'	Ti	\

4. A <u>period</u> is one row in the periodic table. Use <u>period</u> in a sentence.

_____

_____

6
C
12.001

5. A <u>group</u> is a vertical column in the periodic table. Use <u>group</u> in a sentence.

_____

_____

Dr. Birdley Teaches Science –
Elements, Compounds, and Mixtures

Unit 6: The Elements

Contents

NAME:_____

CLASS:_____ DATE:_____

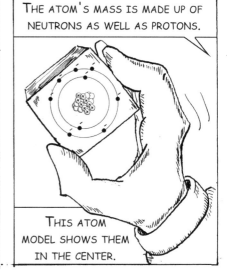

Dr. Birdley Teaches Science –
Elements, Compounds, and Mixtures

SO HERE WE HAVE TWO MAJOR GROUPS OF ELEMENTS; THE ALKALI METALS AND THE NOBLE GASES.

THE ALKALI METALS, LIKE SODIUM, CESIUM, AND FRANCIUM, REACT STRONGLY WITH NON-METALS. THE NOBLE GASES, LIKE NEON AND ARGON, ARE NOT REACTIVE AT ALL!

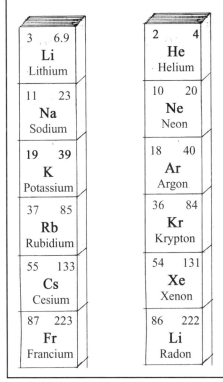

THIS GOES BACK TO WHAT I WAS TALKING ABOUT EARLIER...

EACH VERTICAL GROUP ON THE PERIODIC TABLE CONTAINS ELEMENTS WITH SIMILAR *PROPERTIES*.

3	6.9
Li	
Lithium	

11	23
Na	
Sodium	

19	39
K	
Potassium	

37	85
Rb	
Rubidium	

55	133
Cs	
Cesium	

87	223
Fr	
Francium	

2	4
He	
Helium	

10	20
Ne	
Neon	

18	40
Ar	
Argon	

36	84
Kr	
Krypton	

54	131
Xe	
Xenon	

86	222
Li	
Radon	

THESE GROUPS FORM ON THE PERIODIC TABLE BECAUSE THE ELEMENTS ARE ARRANGED IN ORDER OF ATOMIC NUMBER!

IT'S NEVER TO EARLY FOR THE FUNDAMENTALS.

UH -- OKAY DR. BIRDLEY, BUT IT'S TIME FOR SNACK.

Dr. Birdley Teaches Science –
Elements, Compounds, and Mixtures

ELEMENT BLOCKS, PART 1

Objectives

To establish the meaning of the atomic number and mass number.

Synopsis

Dr. Birdley introduces Jeremiah's daycare teacher to the element blocks.

Main Ideas

1. The atomic number is equal to the number of protons in a single atom.

2. The mass number is equal to the number of protons and neutrons in neutral atoms.

3. Protons and neutrons are located at the center of the atom.

4. The symbols P, N, and E stand for proton, neutron, and electron. They are subatomic particles in an atom.

5. In atoms with no charge, the number of protons is equal to the number of electrons.

6. Each element block shows a specific type of atom.

Vocabulary

Atom	proton	charge
element	neutron	atomic number
nucleus	electron	mass number

Characters

Dr. Birdley, Baby Birdley (Jeremiah), Cindy (Day Care Instructor)

Questions for Discussion

Before Reading:

1. What do you think atoms are made of?

2. What makes elements different?

After Reading:

1. Where is Fluorine on the periodic table?

2. How many blocks would be needed for all the elements of the periodic table?

3. What is the youngest age you think a child could begin learning about the elements and atoms?

4. What are atoms made of?

5. Where are the electrons located?

ELEMENT BLOCKS, PART 2

Objectives

To establish the importance of groups on the periodic table.

Synopsis

At the Beakton Day Care center, Dr. Birdley introduces Jeremiah to the alkali metals and noble gases.

Main Ideas

1. Alkali metals are highly reactive, whereas noble gases are not highly reactive.

2. These two families of elements are represented by vertical groups on the periodic table.

3. Each vertical group on the periodic table contains elements with similar chemical properties.

4. The groups on the periodic table form because the elements are arranged in order of atomic number.

5. Each block contains the element's atomic number, mass number, symbol, and name.

Vocabulary

group	period	reactivity
alkali metal	noble gas	atomic number

Characters

Dr. Birdley, Jeremiah, Cindy

Teacher's Note

It will be helpful to supplement this cartoon with a copy of the periodic table.

Questions for Discussion

Before Reading:

1. How many columns are in the main part of the periodic table? (Exclude the lanthinides and actinides, for the moment)

2. How many periods are on the periodic table?

3. How do scientists categorize elements?

After Reading:

1. What does Dr. Birdley teach Jeremiah?

2. What does Dr. Birdley mean by "groups?"

3. How are groups different from the periods in the periodic table?

Dr. Birdley Teaches Science –
Elements, Compounds, and Mixtures

Study Questions

Directions: Read the related source cartoon and then answer the questions that follow.

1. What element is shown? What information does the block tell you about the element?

_____

_____

2. What does the atomic number tell you about the atom?

_____

_____

3. What does the atomic mass tell you about the atom? Where is most of the atomic mass concentrated?

_____

_____

4. Where are the electrons located in the atom?

_____

_____

5. Three sides of the block were not shown! What information about the element could you put on the other three sides?

_____

_____

Study Questions

Directions: Read the related source cartoon and then answer the questions that follow.

1. How are alkali metals different from noble gases?

_____

_____

2. What is Dr. Birdley's point about the different vertical groups in the periodic table?

_____

_____

3. If you arranged the elements in alphabetical order on the periodic table, would the groups form? Why or why not?

_____

_____

4. The halogens are in a group that is next to the noble gases. They are highly reactive with alkali metals. Look at a periodic table and list five halogens in order from lightest to heaviest.

_____

_____

5. The alkaline earth metals are in a group that is next to the alkali metals. They react with non-metals. Look at a periodic table and list six alkaline earth metals, in order from lightest to heaviest.

_____

_____

NAME:_____

CLASS:_____ DATE:_____

Close-up: Fluorine

Alright, Baby Birdley, this chapter is about **Fluorine**. Fluorine is the most reactive element on earth, and forms compounds with most other elements. In its purest form it is found as a poisonous, corrosive yellow gas, F_2. (Two Fluorine atoms bonded together). Beware! In humid environments it will react with water to form a highly dangerous compound with hydrogen, known as hydroflouric acid (HF).

Fluorine is so reactive that it must be stored in steel containers. Why is this? It badly wants to **gain** an electron in order to complete its outer electron shell. Theoretically, Fluorine's outer electron shell should have seven electrons, but all elements are more stable once they have full valence shells, so Fluorine becomes much more stable if it reacts with other elements to gain one more valence electron. When it does react, it does so explosively. **So watch out!**

Despite its volatile nature, Fluorine is found in many useful compounds such as sodium fluoride (NaF), which is in toothpaste. Fluorine-containing compounds are also found in insecticides and plastics. So useful, yet so dangerous! Well, that's the end of the chapter. Time for bed!

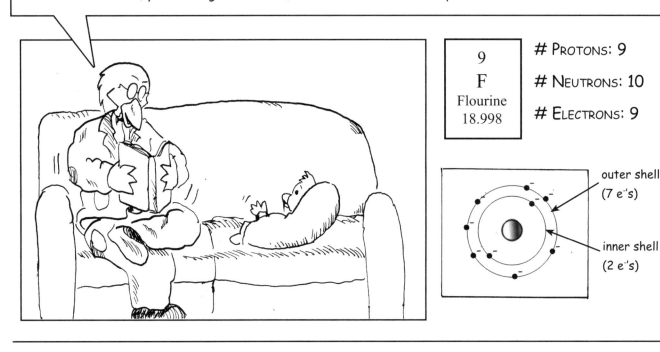

| 9 |
| F |
| Flourine |
| 18.998 |

PROTONS: 9

NEUTRONS: 10

ELECTRONS: 9

outer shell
(7 e⁻'s)

inner shell
(2 e⁻'s)

1. Why is Fluorine so reactive?

_____

_____

2. What are two "real-world" uses of Fluorine? How can it be so dangerous in its elemental form but so useful in compounds?

_____

_____

Dr. Birdley Teaches Science –
Elements, Compounds, and Mixtures

NAME:_____

CLASS:_____DATE:_____

For each element, fill
in the missing information!

KATZ '06

| 2 He Helium 4.0026 | # PROTONS _____ |
| # NEUTRONS _____ |
| # ELECTRONS _____ |

| 7 N Nitrogen 14.007 | # PROTONS _____ |
| # NEUTRONS _____ |
| # ELECTRONS _____ |

| 3 Li Lithium 6.941 | # PROTONS _____ |
| # NEUTRONS _____ |
| # ELECTRONS _____ |

| 9 F Flourine 18.998 | # PROTONS _____ |
| # NEUTRONS _____ |
| # ELECTRONS _____ |

| 6 C Carbon 12.011 | # PROTONS _____ |
| # NEUTRONS _____ |
| # ELECTRONS _____ |

| 19 K Potassium 39.098 | # PROTONS _____ |
| # NEUTRONS _____ |
| # ELECTRONS _____ |

| 29 Cu Copper 63.546 | # PROTONS _____ |
| # NEUTRONS _____ |
| # ELECTRONS _____ |

| 80 Hg Mercury 200.59 | # PROTONS _____ |
| # NEUTRONS _____ |
| # ELECTRONS _____ |

| 50 Sn Tin 118.69 | # PROTONS _____ |
| # NEUTRONS _____ |
| # ELECTRONS _____ |

| 18 Ar Argon 39.948 | # PROTONS _____ |
| # NEUTRONS _____ |
| # ELECTRONS _____ |

THE ELEMENTS

NAME:_____

CLASS:_____ DATE:_____

MAKE YOUR OWN ELEMENT BLOCK!

Directions: Research an element of your choice. Fill in the information below on the element you have selected. Then, cut out the box and close it up. You will have your very own element block!

BASIC INFO

Name:_____

Symbol:_____

Atomic #:_____

Mass #:_____

PHYSICAL PROPERTIES

Phase (rm temp):_____

Density (g/cm^3):_____

Boiling pt:_____

Melting pt:_____

Appearance:_____

FAMILY:_____

GROUP # ____ PD #____

LOCATION (SHADED)

Protons:_____

Neutrons:_____

Electrons:_____

Info on Bonding/Reactivity:

PRESENT IN THESE SUBSTANCES:

ATOMIC MODEL

Dr. Birdley Teaches Science –
Elements, Compounds, and Mixtures

NAME:_____

CLASS:_____DATE:_____

PANEL REVIEW: FLUORINE

Directions: Read the panel in the space below and solve the problems that follow.

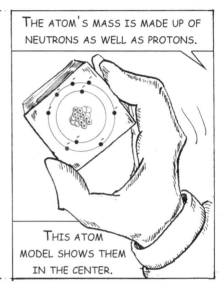

1. How many electrons are in Flourine's inner electron shell? ____

2. How many electrons are in Flourine's outer electron shell? _____

3. If the outer electron shell has a maximum capacity of eight electrons,
   how many electrons does Flourine need to gain to achieve a full outer shell?____

4. How many positive protons does a neutral Flourine atom have? ____

5. How many negative electrons (total) does neutral Flourine atom have? ____

6. If each electron has a charge of -1, what charge would the Flourine atom have
   if it filled its outer shell by obtaining the required number of electrons? ____

7. Using the periodic table, find the other elements in Flourine's vertical "group":

   _____

8. Sodium and the other elements in its "group" bond easily with Flourine.
   List these elements in sodium's group.

   _____

Dr. Birdley Teaches Science –
Elements, Compounds, and Mixtures

NAME:_____

CLASS:_____DATE:_____

MINI-COMIC: GALLIUM

Directions: Read the panels in the space below and answer the questions that follow.

How could Mendeleev have predicted the properties of an element before it had been discovered? He knew that one could predict the position of an element on the periodic table can reveal quite a bit about its properties...even if you have never seen it. On his periodic table, Mendeleev noticed a blank square after Zinc (65). He predicted that an element would eventually be discovered that would fill this square. He called it eka-aluminum and predicted its atomic weight would be 68.

Because elements in the same group have similar characteristics, Mendeleev reasoned that eka-aluminum's properties would be similar to those of the elements above and below the blank square. When Gallium was discovered, it turned out that his predictions were accurate. Although its atomic mass was slightly higher than eka-aluminum's, the reactivity, solubility, and melting point of Gallium was strikingly similar to eka-aluminum's.

1. How did Mendeleev use the periodic table to predict the properties of Gallium before it was discovered?

2. How does this demonstrate the usefulness of the periodic table?

Dr. Birdley Teaches Science –
Elements, Compounds, and Mixtures

Review Unit: Structure of the Atom

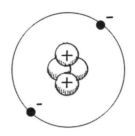

Contents

NAME:_____

CLASS:_____ DATE:_____

PARTICLE	MASS (amu)	CHARGE
PROTON	1	+1
NEUTRON	1	0
ELECTRON	1/1836	1

Dr. Birdley Teaches Science –
Elements, Compounds, and Mixtures

Objectives

1. To identify the three major subatomic particles.

2. To indicate how the number of subatomic particles determine the identity of an atom.

3. To illustrate the relative mass and charge of each atom.

Synopsis

Dr. Birdley, Jaykes, Gina, and Norman have miniaturized themselves so that they are smaller than an atom. As they float around the atom and explain its parts, Owelle reminds them to explain some additional information.

Main Ideas

1. An atom is made up of protons, neutrons, and electrons.

2. Each element has a unique number of protons, neutrons, and electrons.

3. Protons are positively charged, neutrons have no charge, and electrons are negatively charged.

4. Protons and neutrons each have a mass of 1 atomic mass unit (amu); electrons are considerably smaller and have a mass of 1/1836 amu.

Vocabulary

proton	neutron	electron
mass	charge	element

Characters

Dr. Birdley, Jaykes, Gina, Norman, Owelle

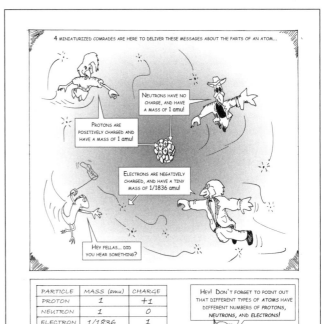

Questions for Discussion

Before Reading:

1. Draw what you think an atom looks like.

2. What do you already know about atoms?

After Reading:

1. What is the smallest subatomic particle?

2. How are Lithium and Hydrogen different in terms of their number of protons? neutrons? electrons?

3. What two particles primarily determine the mass of the atom?

Dr. Birdley Teaches Science –
Elements, Compounds, and Mixtures

Background: Protons, Neutrons, and Electrons

Do you know what it's like to be the size of a subatomic particle?? I didn't think so. Around here the electrons fly around so fast I can barely see them. The size of the nucleus relative to the electron cloud can be likened to the size of a marble in a football stadium. Oddly enough though, the electron's mass (1/1836 amu) is far smaller than that of a proton or neutron (1 amu).

I see that I'm near the nucleus right now. All the mass is basically concentrated here. As I get closer to the nucleus, things seem to get more positive. That's because the nucleus is partially made up of protons, each of which has a charge of +1. Each electron has a charge of -1, so equal numbers of protons and electrons make a neutral atom. The neutrons make up the mass as well but have no charge.

How odd to be hanging out with the three subatomic particles of the atom: the protons, neutrons, and electrons. Every type of atom is made up of these types of particles (although hydrogen has no neutrons). The number of particles determines the properties of the element!

PARTICLE	MASS (amu)	CHARGE
PROTON	1	+1
NEUTRON	1	0
ELECTRON	1/1836	1

Hydrogen   Helium   Lithium

1. Protons have a positive charge of +1 and electrons have a charge of -1. So why are so many atoms neutral?

_____

_____

2. Some atoms, called isotopes, have extra neutrons. If carbon-13 has an atomic mass of 13 amu, how many neutrons does it have? ____

3. Compare the size of the nucleus to the size of the electron cloud. _____

_____

Dr. Birdley Teaches Science –
Elements, Compounds, and Mixtures

Name:_____
Class:_____Date:_____

Study Questions

Directions: Read the related source cartoon and then answer the questions that follow.

1. What are two ways an electron is different from a proton?

_____

_____

2. What two particles are in the nucleus? How are they different?

_____

_____

3. How is the nucleus of a Helium atom different from the nucleus of a lithium atom?

_____

_____

4. What else do you notice about how atoms of different elements are different?

_____

_____

5. Carbon has an atomic mass of 12 and six protons. How many neutrons does it have? How can you tell?

_____

_____

Dr. Birdley Teaches Science –
Elements, Compounds, and Mixtures

Mini-Comic: Valence Electrons

Directions: Read the panels in the space below and answer the questions that follow.

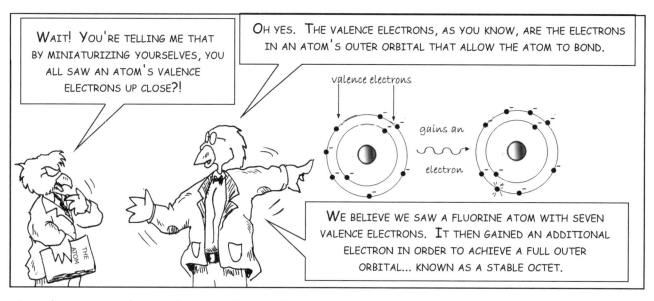

1. Where are valence electrons located?

2. What is the function of a valence electron?

3. Why did the Fluorine atom "want" to gain a valence electron?

4. What is a stable octet?

5. Based on the illustration of the atom on the right, what is the maximum number of electrons that the outer orbital can hold?

6. How about the inner orbital?

THE PARTS OF THE ATOM

NAME:_____

CLASS:_____DATE:_____

LABEL THE PARTS OF THE ATOM IN THE SPACE BELOW! USE THE WORD BANK! BE CAREFUL!

WORD BANK

NUCLEUS	INNER ORBITAL
PROTON	OUTER ORBITAL
NEUTRON	STABLE OCTET
ELECTRON	LITHIUM
VALENCE ELECTRON	NEON

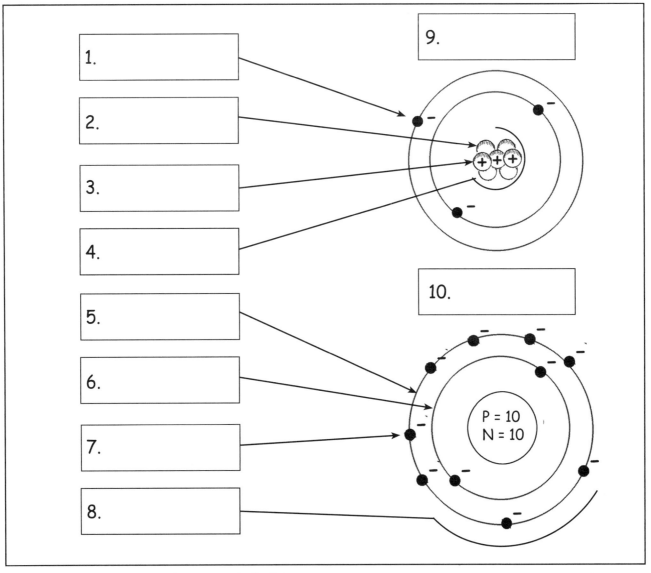

1.

2.

3.

4.

5.

6.

7.

8.

9.

10.

Dr. Birdley Teaches Science –
Elements, Compounds, and Mixtures

Name:_____
Class:_____Date:_____

Vocabulary Build-up!

Directions: Use the following underlined words in sentences that convey their meaning.

1. A <u>proton</u> is a positively charge particle in the nucleus of an atom. It has the mass of one atomic mass unit (amu). Use <u>proton</u> in a sentence.

_____

_____

2. <u>Neutrons</u> are particles in the nucleus of an atom with no charge. Each neutron has a mass of one amu. Use <u>neutron</u> in a sentence.

_____

_____

3. <u>Electrons</u> are particles in the orbitals of an atom with a negative charge and a mass of 1/1862 amu. Use <u>electron</u> in a sentence.

_____

_____

4. The <u>nucleus,</u> which contains protons and neutrons, is the positively charged center of the atom. Use <u>nucleus</u> in a sentence.

_____

_____

nucleus

5. An <u>electron cloud</u> is a region of space where electrons are most likely to be found. Use <u>electron cloud</u> in a sentence.

_____

_____

Dr. Birdley Teaches Science –
Elements, Compounds, and Mixtures

Unit 7: Polar and Nonpolar Molecules

Contents

NAME:_____

CLASS:_____ DATE:_____

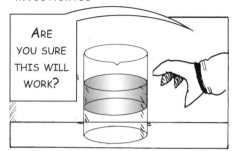

Dr. Birdley Teaches Science –
Elements, Compounds, and Mixtures

NAME:_____

CLASS:_____ DATE:_____

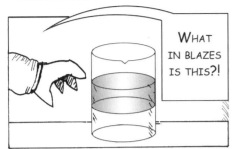

Dr. Birdley Teaches Science—
Elements, Compounds, and Mixtures

A POLAR MOLECULE

Molecular Properties

Objectives

1. To explain why water is a polar molecule.

2. To illustrate how electron distribution can affect the properties of a molecule.

3. To illustrate how the size of an atom can affect the behavior of a molecule's electrons.

Synopsis

Using the zoom glove, Dr. Birdley and Jaykes shrink down to the size of an atom and observe a water molecule up close.

Main Ideas

1. Water molecules (H_2O) are polar molecules in which the hydrogen atoms are partially positive, and oxygen atom is partially negative.

2. Polar molecules have an uneven electron distribution.

3. In polar molecules, atoms that attract electrons more have a high electron affinity, and have a partial negative charge.

4. An atom has a partial negative charge when the negative charge of the electron cloud surrounding the nucleus is greater than the positive charge of its protons.

5. In polar molecules, atoms that have less electron affinity have a partial positive charge.

Vocabulary

polar   electron distribution

nonpolar   partial charge

Characters

Dr. Birdley, Jaykes

Questions for Discussion

Before Reading:

1. What happens when you try to mix oil and water?

2. Why do protons attract electrons?

3. What happens to an atom's charge if there are more electrons than protons in the area?

After Reading:

1. What do Birdley and Jaykes find out about water?

2. If water is polar, what do you suppose oil is? Why?

Dr. Birdley Teaches Science – Elements, Compounds, and Mixtures

Objectives

1. To explain why oil and water do not mix.

2. To provide an example of a nonpolar molecule that exists in oils.

3. To distinguish between polar and nonpolar molecules.

Synopsis

Dean Owelle notices the beaker of oil and water and speculates as to why they do not mix. Birdley and Jaykes, who have been miniaturized and are at the interface between the oil and water, explain the issue.

Main Ideas

1. Oil and water do not mix because oil is nonpolar and water is polar.

2. Polar molecules avoid nonpolar molecules, and vice-versa.

3. Polar molecules have an uneven electron distribution (see previous comic).

4. Nonpolar molecules have an even electron distribution.

5. Pentane (C_5H_{12}) is an example of a non-polar molecule that is found in some oils.

Vocabulary

polar   electron distribution

nonpolar   pentane

Characters

Dr. Birdley, Jaykes, Dean Owelle

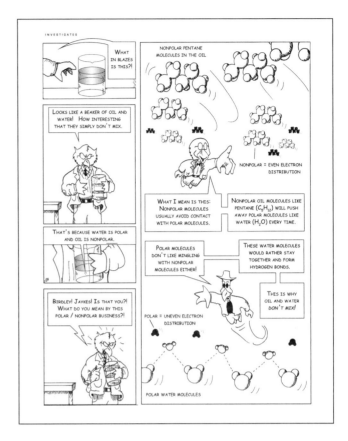

Questions for Discussion

Before Reading:

1. What are some substances that do not mix well with water?

2. What are some substances that do mix with or dissolve in water?

3. What does it reveal about the substance if it does not dissolve in water?

After Reading:

1. Why do oil and water not mix?

2. What are the water molecules doing in the comic?

3. What is the oil molecule in the comic?

Dr. Birdley Teaches Science –
Elements, Compounds, and Mixtures

Study Questions

Directions: Read the related source cartoon and then answer the questions that follow.

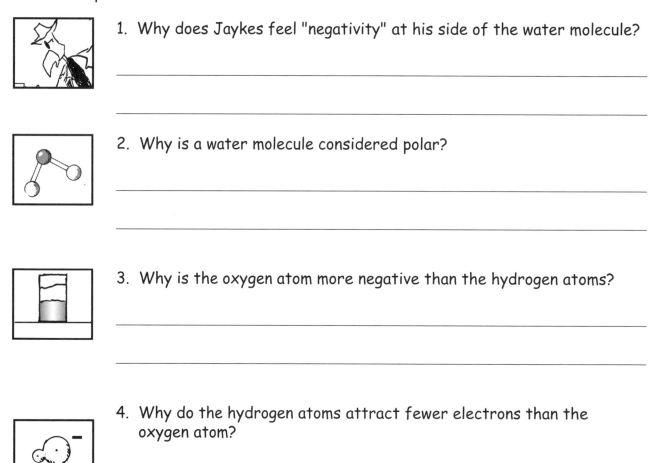

1. Why does Jaykes feel "negativity" at his side of the water molecule?

_____

_____

2. Why is a water molecule considered polar?

_____

_____

3. Why is the oxygen atom more negative than the hydrogen atoms?

_____

_____

4. Why do the hydrogen atoms attract fewer electrons than the oxygen atom?

_____

_____

5. How is the distribution of electrons different in polar and non-polar molecules?

_____

_____

Dr. Birdley Teaches Science –
Elements, Compounds, and Mixtures

OIL AND WATER

Name:_____
Class:_____Date:_____

    Study Questions

Directions: Read the related source cartoon and then answer the questions that follow.

1. According to the comic, what difference between a water molecule and molecules in oil prevents them from interacting?

_____

_____

2. What evidence can you find for this in real life?

_____

_____

3. Based on the comic, where in the beaker are Birdley and Jaykes? (Draw an arrow that points to the correct location and explain why.

_____

_____

4. What is the difference between a polar and nonpolar molecule in terms of how their electrons are distributed?

_____

_____

5. What are two substances that can dissolve in water? Do you predict that they are polar or nonpolar? Why?

_____

_____

Dr. Birdley Teaches Science –
Elements, Compounds, and Mixtures

Background: Polar or Non-Polar?

Here's the deal: nonpolar molecules have an even electron distribution, while polar molecules do not. In polar molecules, electrons cluster around particular atoms, so the molecules develop partial positive and negative charges. (negative "pole" and positive "pole") Look at these examples:

CARBON DIOXIDE

Nonpolar CO_2 is not bent and the symmetrical oxygen atoms allow electrons to be distributed evenly.

HYDROGEN SULFIDE

Polar In H_2S, electrons cluster around the large sulfur atom. Because it is bent, the electron cloud is unevenly distributed, giving the sulfur atom a partial negative charge and the hydrogen atoms partial positive charges.

METHANE

Nonpolar While the carbon atom has six electrons, the hydrogen atoms are evenly spaced around the molecule, resulting in an even electron distribution and no significant partial charges.

CHLOROMETHANE

Polar Unlike CH_4, the chlorine atom in CH_3Cl attracts more electrons than the other hydrogens, so it develops a partial negative charge. The hydrogen atoms become partially positive, and the molecule becomes polar.

1. Why is chloromethane more polar than methane?_____

_____

_____

2. Why is carbon dioxide less polar than hydrogen sulfide?_____

_____

_____

Dr. Birdley Teaches Science –
Elements, Compounds, and Mixtures

Background: Polar or Nonpolar?
PART 2

A few tips on identifying molecules as polar or nonpolar. For polar types, keep your eyes out for bent molecules, where a large electron might be attracting large numbers of electrons. If a molecule is totally symmetrical and has no large atoms that serve as "electron magnets," then it is likely to be nonpolar. Look at these examples:

WATER

Polar In H_2O, electrons cluster around the large oxygen atom. Because it is bent, the electron cloud is unevenly distributed, giving the oxygen atom a partial negative charge and the hydrogen atoms partial positive charges.

HYDROGEN GAS

Nonpolar As with other diatomic gases (gases made up of two of the same element), H_2 is only made up of two identical atoms, each with the same number of electrons. This structure allows electrons to be distributed evenly.

AMMONIA

Polar The nitrogen atom in ammonia attracts more electrons than the hydrogen atoms, so it develops a partial negative charge. The hydrogen atoms become partially positive, so the molecule is polar.

BENZENE

Nonpolar Benzene has evenly spaced hydrogen and carbon atoms. Because the molecule has this type of shape, the electrons end up being evenly distributed across the ring-shaped structure, resulting in no partial charges.

1. Why is hydrogen gas less polar than water?_____

_____

_____

2. Suppose you substituted a chlorine atom for a hydrogen atom on the benzene molecule. (Draw it!) Would the molecule become polar or non-polar? Why?

_____

_____

Dr. Birdley Teaches Science –
Elements, Compounds, and Mixtures

POLAR OR NONPOLAR?

IDENTIFY EACH MOLECULE AS POLAR OR NONPOLAR.

REMEMBER THAT AN ELEMENT'S ATOMIC NUMBER IS EQUAL TO THE NUMBER OF ELECTRONS IT HAS (ASSUMING NO CHARGE).

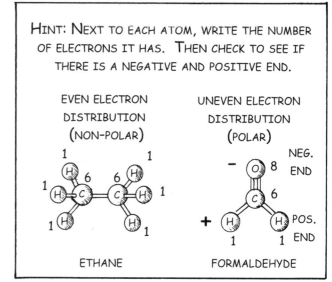

HINT: NEXT TO EACH ATOM, WRITE THE NUMBER OF ELECTRONS IT HAS. THEN CHECK TO SEE IF THERE IS A NEGATIVE AND POSITIVE END.

EVEN ELECTRON DISTRIBUTION (NON-POLAR)

UNEVEN ELECTRON DISTRIBUTION (POLAR)

ETHANE

FORMALDEHYDE

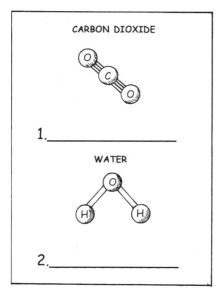

CARBON DIOXIDE

1._____

WATER

2._____

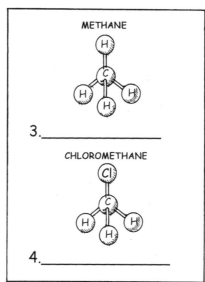

METHANE

3._____

CHLOROMETHANE

4._____

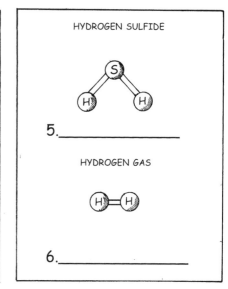

HYDROGEN SULFIDE

5._____

HYDROGEN GAS

6._____

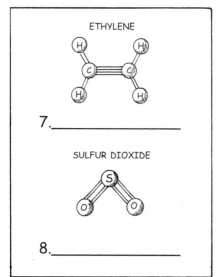

ETHYLENE

7._____

SULFUR DIOXIDE

8._____

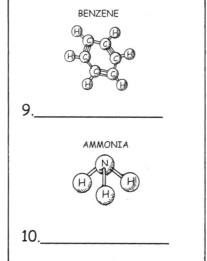

BENZENE

9._____

AMMONIA

10._____

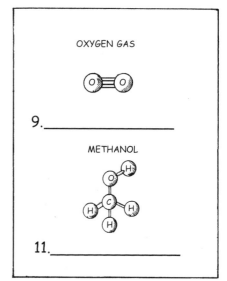

OXYGEN GAS

9._____

METHANOL

11._____

Dr. Birdley Teaches Science –
Elements, Compounds, and Mixtures

Vocabulary Build-up!

Directions: Use the following underlined words in sentences that convey their meaning.

1. A <u>polar molecule</u> has regions that are partially positive, and those that are partially negative. Use <u>polar molecule</u> in a sentence.

_____

_____

2. An <u>electron cloud</u> is the region around an atom or molecule where electrons are most likely to be found. Use <u>electron cloud</u> in a sentence.

_____

_____

3. A <u>nonpolar molecule</u> has an even electron distribution and has no partial charges. Use <u>nonpolar</u> in a sentence.

_____

_____

4. Substances that are <u>insoluble</u> in water will not dissolve readily in water, and contain nonpolar molecules. Use <u>insoluble</u> in a sentence.

_____

_____

5. <u>Distribution</u> describes how things are spaced apart over a given region. In polar molecules, there is an uneven electron distribution. Use <u>distribution</u> in a sentence.

_____

_____

Dr. Birdley Teaches Science –
Elements, Compounds, and Mixtures

Answer Key

Answer Key:

Open-ended questions give science students a chance to make connections between new concepts and their personal experiences, as well as to express their answers in different ways. These questions are one important way to differentiate instruction and address different learning styles. However, open-ended questions do not have a single correct answer, so please read student responses carefully to make sure they are not forming misconceptions. One possible correct answer is always given in this answer key

Page 12: The Language of Chemistry Background Exercise

Molecules are composed of atoms that have bonded together.

Page 13: Symbols and Formulas Study Questions

1. Neil sees the language of chemistry as boring and sees the atomic symbols as a bunch of meaningless letters.
2. The symbols Dr. Birdley points to each stand for a specific element.
3. Atoms combine to form molecules. Birdley illustrates this point using molecular models
4. The goggles enable Neil to see the molecules that compose an object (such as a pencil).
5. Formulas tell us about the types of elements in a molecule, and the number of atoms for each element.

Page 14: Molecules & Formulas Visual Exercise – see p. 93

Page 16: Finding Molecular Mass Mini-Comic

1. 16 amu
2. 30 amu
3. 58 amu
4. 46 amu
5. 81 amu
6. 158 amu
7. 98 amu
8. 131 amu
9. 84 amu
10. 34 amu

Page 17: The Table Method Mini-Comic

Glucose
Carbon: 12, 6, 72
Oxygen: 16, 6, 96
Hydrogen: 1, 12, 12
TOTAL: 24 atoms, 180 amu

Nitrogen (V) Oxide
Nitrogen: 14, 2, 28
Oxygen: 16, 5, 80
TOTAL: 7 atoms, 108 amu

Acetic Acid
Carbon: 12, 2, 24
Oxygen: 16, 1, 16
Hydrogen: 1, 4, 4
TOTAL: 8 atoms, 60 amu

Rust
Iron: 56, 2, 112
Oxygen: 16, 3, 48
TOTAL: 5 atoms, 158 amu

Page 18: The Language of Chemistry Quiz

1. d
2. b
3. d
4. c
5. C_3H_6O
6. b

Element Name	Atomic Mass	# Atoms	Total Mass
Carbon	12	3	36
Oxygen	16	1	16
Hydrogen	1	6	6
TOTAL			58

Page 22: All About Elements Background Exercise

Hydrogen: 1, 1, 1, 0, 1
Carbon: 6, 12, 6, 6, 6
Nitrogen: 7, 14, 7, 7, 7
Lithium: 3, 7, 3, 4, 3
Helium: 2, 4, 2, 2, 2
Fluorine: 9, 19, 9, 10, 9

Page 23: All About Elements Study Questions

1. An element is only made of one type of atom, while a compound or mixture is made of different types of atoms.
2. Atoms are made of protons, neutrons, and electrons. Atoms differ in terms of how many of each particle they have.
3. The number of protons determines the identity of an atom. The atomic number tells you the number of protons in an atom.
4. Carbon has six protons. We know this because carbon's atomic number is six.
5. If an atom is broken apart, it loses its identity.

Page 28: Compound Coolness Background Exercise

Compounds are made of only one type of molecule. Compounds have the same properties, no matter what their size or shape is. Compounds cannot be broken down by physical changes; only by chemical reactions.

Page 29: Compound Coolness Background Exercise

1. In any sample of a compound, you know exactly what it's made of. This is because compounds contain only one type of molecule.
2. Physical properties that do not depend on size include density, melting point, boiling point, and malleability. They depend on composition.
3. A compound can be broken down into its basic elements using a chemical reaction.
4. Within the molecules, the bonds between atoms are broken down and reformed. The result is the formation of new molecules.
5. Compounds are different from elements because they contain more than one type of atom.

Page 30: Compounds: Linking Images
Visual Exercise – see p. 93
Visual Exercise – see p. 93

Page 33: Composition of Matter Study Questions
1. A compound is different from an element because a compound is made of more than one type of atom, while the element is made of only one type of atom.
2. A mixture is different from a compound because a mixture has more than one type of molecule, whereas a compound is made of only one type of molecule.
3. Mixtures cannot be represented by formulas because each type of molecule has a unique formula, and mixtures have more than one type of molecule.
4. The mixture is a gas because all the substances (O_2, CO_2, CH_4) are in gaseous form at room temperature.
5. The only pure element in the mini-comic is Argon, in the first bubble, but the elements that make up the compounds and mixtures include: Nitrogen, Hydrogen, Carbon, and Oxygen.

Page 38: The Nano-Goggles Study Questions
1. Dr. Birdley's goggles allow him to see the molecules that compose a substance or object.
2. Dr. Birdley demonstrates the goggle's powers by identifying the molecules in Owelle's drink as water and carbon dioxide.
3. In the lab cabinet, substance B is a compound because it only has one type of molecule.
4. Compounds consist of only one type of substance; mixtures have multiple types of substances, each with a different chemical composition.
5. Answers will vary; in most cases, answers should refer to the goggle's ability to see what materials, substances, or objects are made of.

Page 39: Two Types of Mixtures Study Questions
1. The beaker on the left contains a heterogeneous mixture, because the substances and objects in the mixture are unevenly distributed.
2. The flask on the right contains the homogeneous mixture, because the substances are evenly distributed.
3. The wide-mouthed jar probably holds the more dense compound. In order to get the compound into the narrow mouth it would need to flow.
4. You could make the heterogeneous mixture more homogeneous by crushing the rock-like objects and then shake or stir the mixture.

Page 40: Two Types of Mixtures / Solutions Background Exercise
While a compound is made of only one type of molecule, a mixture is made up of more than one type of molecule.

Page 42: Element, Compound, or Mixture?
Visual Exercise – see p. 93
Visual Exercise – see p. 93

Page 43: Solutions Mini-Comic
1. The solute is salt (NaCl) and the solvent is water (H_2O).
2. A solution becomes saturated when the maximum amount of solute that could be dissolved into the solvent has been added.
3. A is supersaturated because a layer of undissolved salt has settled at the bottom.
4. To make sure all of the solute dissolves, you would add more water.

Page 44: Elements, Compounds, and Mixtures Graphic Organizer

Elements	Compounds	Mixtures
Helium	Calcium Carbonate	Salt Water
Nickel	Acetone	Vinegar
Boron	Formaldehyde	Mud
Hydrogen Gas	Chalk	Clay
Nitrogen	Sodium Acetate	Pond Water
Mercury	Lithium Chloride	Glucose Solution
Iodine	Baking Soda	Cookie Dough
	Acedic Acid	Taco Sauce
		Acid Rain

Page 45: Matter Concept Map
1. Matter
2. Elements
3. Compound
4. Atom
5. Molecule
6. Mixtures
7. Homogeneous
8. Heterogeneous (7 and 8 are interchangeable.)

Page 46: Elements, Compounds, and Mixtures Quiz
Unit 2-3 Answers
1. a. mixture
   b. compound
   c. element
   d. compound
2. a. compound
   b. mixture
   c. element
   d. compound
   e. element
   f. mixture
   g. element
   h. compound
   i. mixture
3. The mixture would become more homogeneous, because stirring makes the molecules become more evenly distributed throughout the mixture. If all the salt dissolved, the mixture would become a solution.
4. a. homogeneous
   b. heterogeneous.

Page 52: Mendeleev, Part 1 Study Questions
1. Mendeleev is known as the father of the periodic table. He conducted his research at the University of St. Petersburg in Russia.
2. By 1869, Mendeleev knew of over 44 elements and was working on ways to organize them. Birdley thought this was significant because he was laying the groundwork for the modern periodic table.
3. Mendeleev's periodic table was smaller than the one we know today because there were many elements that had not yet been discovered.

4. Answers may vary. Mendelev did not know how many total elements there were to place on the periodic table. Mendeleev did not know that atoms were made up of protons, neutrons, and electrons.

5. Answers will vary.

Page 53: Mendeleev, Part 2 Study Questions

1. To collect data on each element, Mendeleev needed to isolate and purify it; in other words, separate it from other substances.

2. Mendeleev organized the elements by atomic weight.

3. Mendeleev found that in each row, there was a similar pattern to the order in which certain types of elements showed up. This resulted in vertical groups with similar properties.

4. The periodic table is periodic because of the repetitious nature of each period. There is a similar sequence of element types in each row.

5. Whereas Mendeleev organized the elements by atomic weight, we organize them by atomic number.

Page 54: Mendeleev's Table Background Exercise

1. Mendeleev isolated and purified all the elements he could. He then learned about their properties and atomic masses. He then wrote their properties on notecards and arranged them in order of atomic mass. Finally, he constructed a table so that its vertical columns had the same properties.

2. Whereas today's periodic table has 110 elements, Mendeleev's periodic table only had 63. While today's periodic table has the elements arranged in order of atomic number, Mendeleev's table has them arranged in order of atomic mass. Among the missing elements in 1869 were gallium and the inert gases.

Page 55: Mendeleev's Table in 1869
Visual Exercise – see p. 93

Visual Exercise – see p. 93

Page 62: Element Blocks, Part 1 Study Questions

1. The block tells you about the atomic mass, atomic number, name, symbol, numbers of subatomic particles. It also gives you a diagram of the atom.

2. The atomic number tells you how many protons the atom has.

3. The atomic mass tells you about how many protons and neutrons are in the atom. Most of the atomic mass is concentrated in the nucleus.

4. Electrons are located outside the nucleus.

5. Answers will vary. They could include physical properties (boiling point, melting point, density, etc.), human applications, and where it is found.

Page 63: Element Blocks, Part 2 Study Questions

1. Whereas alkali metals are very reactive, noble gases are not reactive at all.

2. Dr. Birdley's point is that each vertical group has elements with similar properties.

3. If you were to arrange the elements in alphabetical order, they would not be organized in groups with similar properties. Organizing the elements by atomic number facilitates this.

4. The halogens include fluorine, chlorine, bromine, iodine, and astatine.

5. The alkali metals include beryllium, magnesium, calcium, strontium, barium, and radon.

Page 65: Element Analysis Visual Exercise – see p. 94

Element Analysis Visual Exercise – see p. 94

Page 64: Fluorine Close-up

1. Fluorine is highly reactive because it almost has a full outer shell (7 out of 8 electrons), and will readily bond with other elements in order to gain an additional electron.

2. Fluorine is used in toothpaste, plastics, and pesticides. It is dangerous in its elemental form because it is unstable. When it bonds with an element to form a compound, it gains an electron and becomes stable.

Page 67: Fluorine Panel Review

1. 2 electrons (inner shell)
2. 7 electrons (outer shell)
3. It needs to gain one electron to achieve a stable outer shell
4. 9 protons
5. 9 electrons
6. A Fluorine ion would have a charge of -1
7. Elements in Fluorine's "group:" Chlorine, Bromine, Iodine, and Astanine
8. Elements in Sodium's "group:" Lithium, Potassium, Rubidium, Cesium, and Francium

Page 68: Gallium Mini-Comic

1. Mendeleev predicted the properties of Gallium based on its position on the periodic table. He predicted that its properties would be similar to the elements in its vertical group.

2. Mendeleev's successful prediction illustrates that the periodic table provides information on an element's chemical properties simply by showing which group it belongs in.

Page 72: Protons, Neutrons, & Electrons Background Exercise

1. Atoms are neutral because even though they are made up of charged particles, they have equal numbers of positively and negatively charged particles, so the overall charge still adds up to zero.

2. Carbon-13 has 7 neutrons. The 7 neutrons plus the 6 protons create the mass of 13 amu.

3. The nucleus is a great deal smaller than the electron cloud. If the electron cloud were as large as a football stadium, the nucleus would be the size of a marble.

Page 73: Subatomic Particles Study Questions

1. Protons have a charge of +1 and a mass of 1 amu, electrons have a charge of -1 and 1/1836 amu.

2. The two particles in the nucleus are protons and neutrons. Whereas neutrons are neutral and have no charge, protons have a positive charge.

3. The nucleus of a helium atom has two protons and two neutrons. The nucleus of a lithium atom has 3 protons and 4 neutrons.

4. Answers will vary but may indicate that different atoms have different numbers of orbitals and/or electrons.

5. Because the nucleus is made up of protons and neutrons, and each neutron has a mass of one, then carbon must have six neutrons.

Page 74: Valence Electrons Mini-Comic

1. Valence electrons are located in the outer shell of the atom.

2. The valence electrons enable the atoms to bond with other atoms.

3. The Fluorine atom "wanted" to gain an electron to complete its outer shell.

4. A stable octet is a valence shell that is full of electrons.
5. The maximum number of electrons that the outer orbital can hold is eight.
6. The maximum number of electrons that the inner orbital can hold is two.

Page 75: The Parts of the Atom Visual Exercise
– see p. 94

Page 82: Polar and Nonpolar Molecules
Study Questions
1. Jaykes feels negativity because of the partial negative charge on the oxygen atom.
2. A water molecules is considered polar because its oxygen atom has a partial negative charge and its hydrogen atoms have partial positive charges.
3. The oxygen atom is more negative than the hydrogen atoms because it has more electrons surrounding it.
4. While the oxygen atom has eight protons, each hydrogen atom only has one proton. As a result, the hydrogen atom attracts fewer electrons than the hydrogen atoms.
5. Electrons are more evenly distributed in nonpolar molecules than in polar molecules.

Page 83: Oil and Water Study Questions
1. The difference that prevents oil and water from interacting is that molecules in oil are nonpolar while water molecules are polar.
2. Examples may vary. Beads of water form on oily spots in a driveway. An oil spill in the ocean does not mix with the water.
3. Because Birdley is swimming among pentane molecules and Jaykes is swimming among water molecules, they must be at the interface between the oil and water.
4. Polar molecules have an uneven electron distribution while nonpolar molecules have an even electron distribution.
5. Two substances that can dissolve in water are sugar and salt. They are polar because they can interact with water molecules.

Page 84: Polar or Non-Polar, Part 1
Background Exercise
1. Chloromethane is more polar than methane because the chlorine atom attracts more electrons than the hydrogens, creating a partial negative charge near the chlorine atom.
2. Carbon dioxide is less polar than hydrogen disulfide because its electrons are more evenly distributed. This is mainly due to its unbent shape and its symmetry.

Page 85: Polar or Non-Polar, Part 2
Background Exercise
1. Hydrogen gas is less polar than water because all of its atoms are the same. Water not only has different atoms, but the oxygen atom attracts electrons towards it and away from the hydrogens, giving the area around the oxygen atom a partial negative charge.
2. If you substituted a chlorine atom for a hydrogen atom, the molecule would be polar, because the electrons would cluster around the larger (and more positive) chlorine atom, creating an uneven electron distribution. (The drawing should look the same as the molecule except any one "H" could be replaced with a "Cl.")

Page 86: Polar or Nonpolar Visual Exercise
– see p. 94

Page 14 Molecules & Formulas

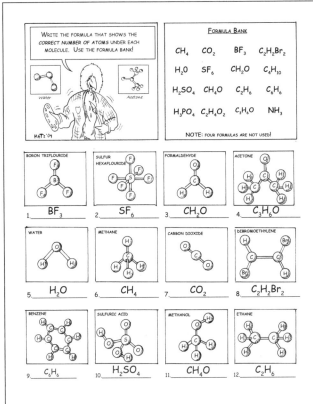

WRITE THE FORMULA THAT SHOWS THE *CORRECT NUMBER OF ATOMS* UNDER EACH MOLECULE. USE THE FORMULA BANK!

Water   Acetone

KATZ '04

FORMULA BANK

CH_4 CO_2 BF_3 $C_2H_2Br_2$

H_2O SF_6 CH_2O C_4H_{10}

H_2SO_4 CH_4O C_2H_6 C_6H_6

H_3PO_4 $C_2H_4O_2$ C_3H_6O NH_3

NOTE: FOUR FORMULAS ARE NOT USED!

BORON TRIFLOURIDE
1. BF_3

SULFUR HEXAFLOURIDE
2. SF_6

FORMALDEHYDE
3. CH_2O

ACETONE
4. C_3H_6O

WATER
5. H_2O

METHANE
6. CH_4

CARBON DIOXIDE
7. CO_2

DIBROMOETHYLENE
8. $C_2H_2Br_2$

BENZENE
9. C_6H_6

SULFURIC ACID
10. H_2SO_4

METHANOL
11. CH_4O

ETHANE
12. C_2H_6

Page 30 Compounds: Linking Images

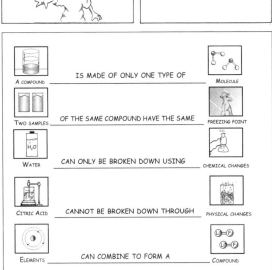

IN THE SPACE BETWEEN EACH SET OF IMAGES, WRITE A LINKING PHRASE TO CREATE A FACTUAL SENTENCE. USE THE PHRASE BANK!

PHRASE BANK

CANNOT BE BROKEN DOWN THROUGH

IS MADE OF ONLY ONE TYPE OF

CAN ONLY BE BROKEN DOWN USING

OF THE SAME COMPOUND HAVE THE SAME

CAN COMBINE TO FORM A

A COMPOUND — IS MADE OF ONLY ONE TYPE OF — MOLECULE

TWO SAMPLES — OF THE SAME COMPOUND HAVE THE SAME — FREEZING POINT

WATER — CAN ONLY BE BROKEN DOWN USING — CHEMICAL CHANGES

CITRIC ACID — CANNOT BE BROKEN DOWN THROUGH — PHYSICAL CHANGES

ELEMENTS — CAN COMBINE TO FORM A — COMPOUND

Page 42 Element, Compound, or Mixture?

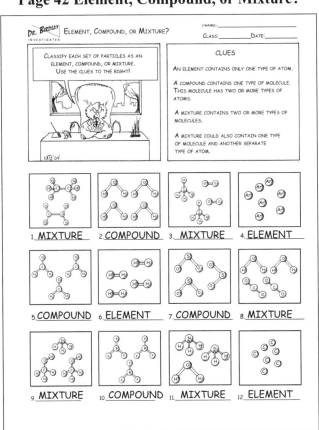

DR. BIRDLEY INVESTIGATES | ELEMENT, COMPOUND, OR MIXTURE?

NAME: _____
CLASS: _____ DATE: _____

CLASSIFY EACH SET OF PARTICLES AS AN ELEMENT, COMPOUND, OR MIXTURE. USE THE CLUES TO THE RIGHT!

KATZ '04

CLUES

AN ELEMENT CONTAINS ONLY ONE TYPE OF ATOM.

A COMPOUND CONTAINS ONE TYPE OF MOLECULE. THIS MOLECULE HAS TWO OR MORE TYPES OF ATOMS.

A MIXTURE CONTAINS TWO OR MORE TYPES OF MOLECULES.

A MIXTURE COULD ALSO CONTAIN ONE TYPE OF MOLECULE AND ANOTHER SEPARATE TYPE OF ATOM.

1. MIXTURE   2. COMPOUND   3. MIXTURE   4. ELEMENT

5. COMPOUND   6. ELEMENT   7. COMPOUND   8. MIXTURE

9. MIXTURE   10. COMPOUND   11. MIXTURE   12. ELEMENT

Page 55 Mendeleev's Table in 1869

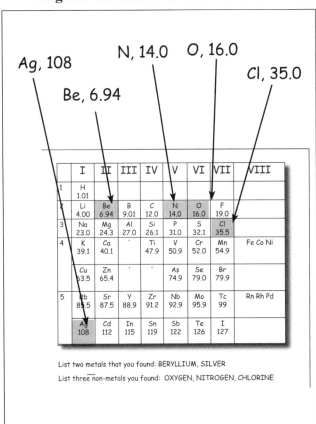

Ag, 108

Be, 6.94

N, 14.0

O, 16.0

Cl, 35.0

	I	II	III	IV	V	VI	VII	VIII
1	H 1.01							
2	Li 4.00	Be 6.94	B 9.01	C 12.0	N 14.0	O 16.0	F 19.0	
3	Na 23.0	Mg 24.3	Al 27.0	Si 26.1	P 31.0	S 32.1	Cl 35.5	
4	K 39.1	Ca 40.1	'	Ti 47.9	V 50.9	Cr 52.0	Mn 54.9	Fe Co Ni
	Cu 63.5	Zn 65.4	'		As 74.9	Se 79.0	Br 79.9	
5	Rb 85.5	Sr 87.5	Y 88.9	Zr 91.2	Nb 92.9	Mo 95.9	Tc 99	Rn Rh Pd
	Ag 108	Cd 112	In 115	Sn 119	Sb 122	Te 126	I 127	

List two metals that you found: BERYLLIUM, SILVER

List three non-metals you found: OXYGEN, NITROGEN, CHLORINE

93

Dr. Birdley Teaches Science –
Elements, Compounds, and Mixtures

Page 65 Element Analysis

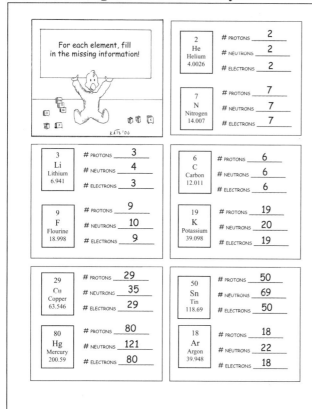

For each element, fill in the missing information!

2 He Helium 4.0026	# PROTONS	2
	# NEUTRONS	2
	# ELECTRONS	2

7 N Nitrogen 14.007	# PROTONS	7
	# NEUTRONS	7
	# ELECTRONS	7

3 Li Lithium 6.941	# PROTONS	3
	# NEUTRONS	4
	# ELECTRONS	3

6 C Carbon 12.011	# PROTONS	6
	# NEUTRONS	6
	# ELECTRONS	6

9 F Flourine 18.998	# PROTONS	9
	# NEUTRONS	10
	# ELECTRONS	9

19 K Potassium 39.098	# PROTONS	19
	# NEUTRONS	20
	# ELECTRONS	19

29 Cu Copper 63.546	# PROTONS	29
	# NEUTRONS	35
	# ELECTRONS	29

50 Sn Tin 118.69	# PROTONS	50
	# NEUTRONS	69
	# ELECTRONS	50

80 Hg Mercury 200.59	# PROTONS	80
	# NEUTRONS	121
	# ELECTRONS	80

18 Ar Argon 39.948	# PROTONS	18
	# NEUTRONS	22
	# ELECTRONS	18

Page 75 The Parts of the Atom

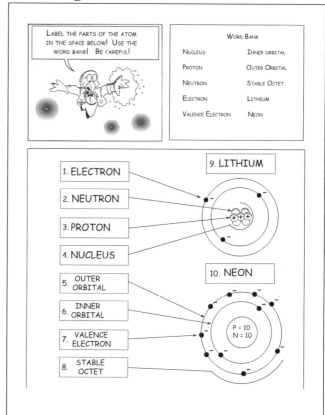

LABEL THE PARTS OF THE ATOM IN THE SPACE BELOW! USE THE WORD BANK! BE CAREFUL!

WORD BANK

NUCLEUS — INNER ORBITAL
PROTON — OUTER ORBITAL
NEUTRON — STABLE OCTET
ELECTRON — LITHIUM
VALENCE ELECTRON — NEON

1. ELECTRON
2. NEUTRON
3. PROTON
4. NUCLEUS
5. OUTER ORBITAL
6. INNER ORBITAL
7. VALENCE ELECTRON
8. STABLE OCTET
9. LITHIUM
10. NEON

P = 10
N = 10

Page. 86 Polar or Nonpolar?

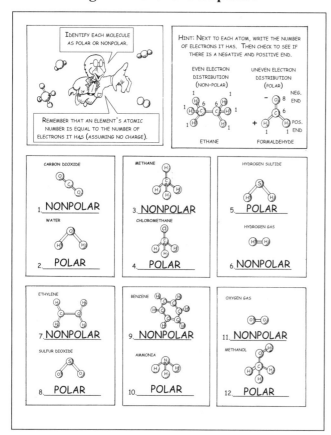

IDENTIFY EACH MOLECULE AS POLAR OR NONPOLAR.

REMEMBER THAT AN ELEMENT'S ATOMIC NUMBER IS EQUAL TO THE NUMBER OF ELECTRONS IT HAS (ASSUMING NO CHARGE).

HINT: NEXT TO EACH ATOM, WRITE THE NUMBER OF ELECTRONS IT HAS. THEN CHECK TO SEE IF THERE IS A NEGATIVE AND POSITIVE END.

EVEN ELECTRON DISTRIBUTION (NON-POLAR)

UNEVEN ELECTRON DISTRIBUTION (POLAR)

ETHANE — FORMALDEHYDE

CARBON DIOXIDE
1. NONPOLAR

METHANE
3. NONPOLAR

HYDROGEN SULFIDE
5. POLAR

WATER
2. POLAR

CHLOROMETHANE
4. POLAR

HYDROGEN GAS
6. NONPOLAR

ETHYLENE
7. NONPOLAR

BENZENE
9. NONPOLAR

OXYGEN GAS
11. NONPOLAR

SULFUR DIOXIDE
8. POLAR

AMMONIA
10. POLAR

METHANOL
12. POLAR

Dr. Birdley Teaches Science – Elements, Compounds, and Mixtures